John Carroll

Effective Time Management

In easy steps is an imprint of In Easy Steps Limited
4 Chapel Court · 42 Holly Walk · Leamington Spa
Warwickshire · United Kingdom · CV32 4YS
www.ineasysteps.com

Notice of Liability
Every effort has been made to ensure that this book contains accurate
and current information. However, In Easy Steps Limited and the
author shall not be liable for any loss or damage suffered by readers
as a result of any information contained herein.

Trademarks
All trademarks are acknowledged as belonging to their respective
companies.

In Easy Steps Limited supports The Forest Stewardship Council (FSC),
the leading international forest certification organisation. All our titles
that are printed on Greenpeace approved FSC certified paper carry the
FSC logo.

MIX
Paper from
responsible sources
FSC® C020837

Printed and bound in the United Kingdom

ISBN 978-1-84078-559-3

Contents

1 Introduction

This chapter provides the background to the need for effective time management. It covers why we never seem to have enough time and how we can begin to find it.

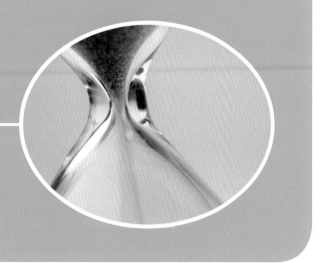

Effective Time Management

Most of us have problems with time management and many of us, struggling to get our work done, end up working longer and longer hours. But these problems can be resolved. Time management is not about the time you spend working but about the *way* you spend your time working. Production line workers have very little choice about what they do but as managers and knowledge workers we can choose how to spend our time.

The Problem

Over the years the problems we face seem to have got worse rather than better. Pagers gave way to mobile phones and smart phones. Memos gave way to emails and texts. The telephone gave way to social networking and tweeting. Computers gave way to laptops and tablets. Diaries gave way to organizers and personal digital assistants. All of these new innovations seem to bring new challenges in effectively managing our time. There just seems to be too much to do and too little time in which to do it in.

Even home-working, the 'Holy Grail' for many people, turns out to bring as many additional problems as it solves. And of course with the concept of 'open door' management (even if you close the door) people will stick their heads round the door with just another quick question for you.

The Solution

The solution is of course not to work 'harder' but to work 'smarter' and manage your time more effectively. This book is called **Effective Time Management in easy steps**:

- Time Management: will show you how you really can manage your time

- Effective: by identifying the real priorities and doing the right things at the right time

- In Easy Steps: the topics in the book are set out in simple steps to show you how best to implement them

Efficiency is about doing things quickly and correctly and it should result in you being more productive. Effectiveness is about working smarter and it can produce the greatest rewards when it comes to managing time. Effectiveness can result in substantial benefits to you and your organization. While this book will identify some efficiency savings it will concentrate on effectiveness.

Effective Time Management

This book is arranged as a series of topics, each of which will address one particular aspect of time management. Each of these is valuable in its own right but together they build into a system that will allow you to get the best out of your time, both at work and at leisure.

The approach of this book is to work through a series of detailed topics, in easy steps. In summary they are:

1. First you need to develop a clear understanding about what you choose to spend your time on now

2. Next you should identify (and document) your goals for what you want to achieve in life

3. Then you need to develop a plan for how you will go about achieving them. First by developing a long term plan, then a mid term plan and finally a daily plan

4. When you get down to the daily plan, you need to build in chunks of time to deal with the things which you know will happen and will require your time

5. Then prioritize what you will choose to do, so that you always work on the most important tasks first and schedule these into your day plan

6. At the end of each day you should review what you actually did during the day, learn any lessons from it and use it to plan the next day

7. Finally you need to review your progress at the strategic level from time to time in order to measure your progress towards achieving your overall goals

These are the seven steps to effective time management that will be developed and expanded through the rest of the book. They are also the seven steps to developing your potential and achieving your long term goals.

Hot tip

Work through the first three chapters as they set the guidelines for developing effective time management.

Why Time Management?

Why do we need time management, effective or otherwise? The best place to start is by looking at some of the challenges we face in our everyday life.

The Challenges

These are the typical problems that we face and have to deal with in our day-to-day working life:

- Changing priorities: no matter how carefully we try to control what we are working on, the demands of the business can mean a sudden change of priority over which we may have little control

- Crisis management: often referred to as fire-fighting and usually introduced with a cry of "drop everything and man the pumps!"

- Trying to do too much: we all like to help people and this often results in us trying to do more than we should (see also Chapter 6 Saying No)

- Telephone interruptions: the phone rings, we pick it up and reply and no matter how short the call, we then have to work our way back to what we were doing before

- Drop-in visitors: as for telephone interruptions, these have a much bigger impact than the time of the interruption

- Ineffective delegation: if we don't delegate effectively we are making a rod for our own backs and may still end up having to do the work ourselves

- Cluttered desk/losing things: if we don't keep our workspace organized we will waste precious time trying to find things

- Lack of self-discipline: we are our own worst enemies; we know what we should be doing but somehow end up doing something else

- Procrastination: again we choose to put things off until later at our peril

- An inability to say no: particularly to our friends or boss

- Endless meetings: rushing from one meeting to another is a sure sign that things are out of control

So those are the sorts of challenges we face and the best way to deal with them is by developing better time awareness.

Time Awareness

This book will show you how to develop that better time awareness through a process of:

1   Understanding how (and perhaps more importantly why) you choose to spend your time as you do now

2   Identifying and eliminating any current time wasting activities that prevent you from doing the things that really matter

3   Planning to make the best possible use of the time that is available to you

4   Learning how to set achievable goals and developing the plans that will allow you to meet them

5   Learning how to delegate effectively and control the process of delegation for your own benefit and that of the people you delegate to

6   Learning techniques to manage interruptions, clear the clutter and get yourself organized

7   Making time available in your daily schedule to allow you to think creatively

8   Finding time to relax and enjoy life both at work and outside of it

9   Developing a personal action plan that will bring it all together and allow you to achieve your time management goals and life plans

Follow this process through the book to maximize your effective time management.

The Paradox of Time

Have you ever found yourself thinking something like:

"I'd like to be able to manage my time better but I can never seem to find the time to do it!"

Well, picking up this book is the first step in that process. This book will show you exactly how to do it in easy steps.

We Can't Manage Time

The first thing to say is that time management is not about managing time itself. No one can do that, even Albert Einstein could not manage time, just study it. Time management is about managing the way we spend the time that is available to us.

Poor Time Management

There's a real need for effective time management because poor time management can leave us feeling very frustrated at the end of the working day. Things don't get completed and we carry them forward on an ever-extending To Do list. Or worse still we end up taking them home with us to work on later but when we try to do it we find we can't concentrate.

The longer we work without adequate breaks to rest, relax and recharge our batteries, the poorer the quality of the work that we do becomes. Our effectiveness goes way down. The To Do list gets longer and longer and all of this produces stress. Does any of this sound familiar?

Symptoms

We looked at some of the challenges we face in the previous topic but some of these challenges are actually symptoms of things that are wrong. Things such as:

- Crisis Management - Rushing from one problem to the next and responding to the latest, most urgent crisis is a symptom of someone who is out of control of their time. It is not only stressful for them it is also stressful for everyone else around them.

- Being at Everyone's Beck and Call - The more we look after other people the more dependent on us they become. We try to help people but we can end up doing their work for them as well as trying to do our own work! This is a real lose-lose situation.

- On a Treadmill - We can find ourselves on some sort of treadmill where we just keep on struggling uphill but seem to get nowhere. This situation not only causes frustration but becomes very stressful. The problem is we just keep on doing things out of a sense of responsibility or habit.

The Plan

We need to break the mould and decide how we can use our time most effectively for our organization and ourselves:

1. Start now: there is no time like the present and if you put it off until you are ready, you never will be (see the comments on procrastination on page 24)

2. Be fully committed: this exercise is going to change your life and if you go at it in a half-hearted manner it will never work out

3. Set your goal: if you don't have a clear objective you will never be able to achieve it

4. Make a plan: if you don't have a plan you will never get to achieve your goal

5. Watch yourself: if you start to identify any of the symptoms of poor time management, review where you are and reappraise what you are trying to achieve

6. See it through: you can pick and choose the topics that address your greatest needs but if you don't work right through your plan, you will never reach your goal

7. Include life outside work: we spend around one third of our life sleeping, one third working and one third relaxing and being with our loved ones. All three are equally important for a happy and successful life

Follow these steps and you will escape from the paradox of time and begin a happier and more successful life.

Beware

Do not neglect the other two thirds of your life as it is equally if not more important than work!

What is Time?

We know there are 60 seconds in a minute, 60 minutes in an hour, 24 hours in a day, 365 days in a year (occasionally 366) and, with luck, 70+ years in a lifetime. There is absolutely no point in trying to change any of that. Time is fixed and we cannot change it. All we can do is try to use it more effectively.

Time Seems to Change

Interestingly time does seem to speed up and slow down:

- Remember when you were young how time seemed to go so slowly? The summers seemed to last forever but unfortunately so too did the school terms

- As we begin to get older time seems to speed up and the years just seem to fly past

But it's not just with age that the passage of time seems to change, consider also:

- When we are busy or enjoying ourselves, time just seems to fly past and suddenly it's time to go and we find ourselves wondering where all the time went

- Conversely when we are bored or waiting for something, time just seems to crawl by. After an eternity of waiting for a bus, train or plane we look at our watch and find only five minutes has elapsed

But time hasn't changed; it is still elapsing at the same rate. What has changed is our perception of the passage of time. So if we can somehow harness this perception to our advantage we can begin to make better use of our time.

Time Management

To make our use of time more effective, we need to consider two aspects of time management. First there are things that we want to do, given that we have the time necessary to do them. Second there are the things we would like to stop doing in order to give us some of that time.

What we Want to Do

The sort of things we want to do are:

- To use our time more effectively so that we can concentrate on doing the things that really matter

- Given the finite amount of time available, we would like to get more done in that available time

- We would very much like to strike the right balance between work and ourselves, friends and loved ones. This is often referred to as "quality of life"

- We would also like to feel in more control of our time and life so that we can concentrate on doing the things that really matter to us

- And perhaps most of all, we want to feel more relaxed about our work and life

Things we Want to Stop Doing

On the other hand we want to stop:

- Any waste of time: as time is so precious and valuable any waste of it is a lost opportunity to do something more meaningful and important

- Forgetting important things that really matter to us; birthdays, anniversaries and any other important events

- Rushing to meet deadlines: particularly when those deadlines are sometimes meaningless to us and often almost impossible to achieve

- Being late for meetings: as we know that means we won't be properly prepared and still worse we may have kept other people, who were on time, waiting

- Feeling out of control: as we know that we are less effective when we are not fully in control

- Feeling stressed: as that not only leads to poor health but we are much more likely to make mistakes when we are in a highly stressed state

So we have two checklists of things we want to do more of and things we want to do less of or stop altogether. If you can do even some of these your time will be spent more effectively. The greater the pressure you are currently under, the greater the benefit of addressing this issue. It follows that effective time management will bring the greatest benefit to people who are busy.

The Cost of Time

We've all heard the business expression "Time is Money" but is it true? In some ways it is, as your time costs the business you work for money. This is true whether you work for an organization or work for yourself. It is certainly true in a production environment where stopping a production process and then having to restart it can be extremely costly in real money terms of lost production or lost customer goodwill.

But is it true in a business management or knowledge worker environment? Consider the following:

- You can always make some more money if you need it but you can't make or buy time; once it has gone it is gone forever

- So perhaps time is actually more valuable than money

- We try to save money in order to invest it wisely for our future benefit

- Perhaps what we need to do is to try and do the same for time and invest it wisely for our future benefit

Working Time Cost

But you can put a cost on your working time, whether you work for an organization or for yourself. In fact if you work for a large organization that uses cross-charging you may already know exactly what your time costs but if not, here is an easy way of calculating it:

1. Take your annual gross salary cost, before any deductions and including the average of any commission or bonus payments that you receive

2. Double it. The resultant figure equates to the cost of employing you in that it allows for the cost of premises, management, taxes and other costs that your employer (or yourself if you are self-employed) also pays to keep you functioning in the business

3. Divide it by 40. That's the average number of fully productive weeks you will work in an average year. This allows for holidays, vacations, sickness, training, attending company meetings and all the other things that eat into

Beware

Most people and their employers believe it's a much bigger number than this!

your time. If you work for an organization that records employees' time for billing purposes and if employees fill in their time sheets honestly you should be able to verify it. The author has been recording his and other employees' time for many years and this is an honest average

4. Divide it by the number of hours you are contracted to work in a week, which should not be more than 40 and hopefully somewhat less in these enlightened times

5. The answer is the cost to your employer (or yourself if you work for yourself) for each hour you work, regardless of how productive you are in that working hour

Here is a worked example of a typical knowledge worker's costs to their employer:

Hourly Cost Calculation

Gross Annual Salary:	$60,000
Cost of Employment Overheads:	$60,000
Total Cost of Employment:	$120,000
Cost of one week's work:	$3,000
Cost of one hour's work:	$75

So that's an example of the real cost to our employers of one hour of our time while we are at work. That is the cost whether we are working productively or not and whether or not what we are doing is bringing any real benefit to the business.

Work out your own real cost per hour and every time you wonder if you should do something or not ask yourself this question: Is what I am about to do worth $75 (or whatever your cost works out to be) per hour to my employer? If the answer turns out to be no, should you be doing it?

Hot tip

Any time you get a salary increase re-work your costs, it will help you keep your feet on the ground!

Accepting Responsibility

If you are going to develop an effective approach to the way you manage your time, the very first thing you must do is to accept responsibility. You are the only person who can do anything about improving your time management. So ask yourself some questions about the way you use your time:

Who's in Control?

Who is really in control of your time? Is it your boss? Is it your subordinates? Is it your co-workers and colleagues?

The answer should be you and only you. Your boss, subordinates and co-workers can all ask you to do things for them and they can ask you to prioritize one piece of work over another but at the end of the day they are not in control of your time. Regardless of what other people may ask you to do, it is you who decides what to do next. So the real question to ask yourself is: are you in control of your time or is time in control of you?

Can you Change?

Having accepted that you are responsible for the way you use your time, the next question to ask yourself is: can you change your approach to the way you use time?

If you want to develop an effective approach to time management the answer has to be yes. If you stop doing the things that waste time and begin to choose the right things to do, you will start to free up your time immediately and be more effective.

Does it Make Sense?

The final question to ask yourself is: does this make sense for you and will it make sense for your organization?

If it does then you are ready to take the first step, which is to define your personal objectives using the form opposite. Be honest with yourself about what you really want to achieve both in terms of your work and your personal life.

SMART Objectives

Objectives should be SMART: Strategic, in that they should really matter; Measurable, so you can track your progress; Agreed with anyone else they impact on; Realistic, as there is no point aiming for something that is completely out of reach; and Timed, as if you don't have a target date they will never be completed.

Personal Objectives

What is your ultimate aim in life?

What is your goal in improving your time management?

What benefits do you think this will bring in your working life?

What benefits do you think this will bring in your private life?

What are the things you want to do more of?

What are the things you want to do less of?

How this Book is Organized

The rest of this book is organized in such a way that you can work your way straight through it but it is also sectioned into chapters that deal with specific topics so you can pick out the areas of most benefit to you.

Chapter 1: Introduction
In this first chapter we have introduced the subject and why we need time management. It has set out a few of the issues and some of the benefits of using more effective time management.

Chapter 2: Time Flies
In chapter two we will look at where all the time goes and some of the common problems we all face. It introduces the importance of developing a time log to record how you currently spend your time, how to analyze it and how you can begin to change the way you work.

Chapter 3: Priorities
Building on the time usage and analysis from the previous chapter we begin to explore the development of long term plans, medium term plans and daily plans. It then explains the most effective way of prioritizing what you actually spend your time on.

Chapter 4: More on Time
Not all time is the same and chapter four explores how you can establish your most productive time in order to use it to the best advantage. It also introduces some other techniques you can use to become more effective.

Chapter 5: Getting Organized
In chapter five we look at organizing your workspace and the way you communicate to make the most effective use of your time. We also look at some of the tools than can help you organize your time more effectively.

Chapter 6: Saying No
No one likes to say no but if you don't learn how to do it correctly you will never be fully effective in managing your time.

Chapter 7: Distractions
In chapter seven we look at the real cost of interruptions and other distractions and how you can minimize their impact by managing them effectively.

Chapter 8: Effective Meetings

We all spend time in meetings and often far too much time. Chapter eight explores how you can make meetings more effective by preparation, controlling the meeting and the all-important follow up, so that everyone benefits.

Chapter 9: Effective Delegation

We can't do everything ourselves so we all need to delegate. We look in this chapter at some of the problems with delegation and how you can learn to delegate effectively.

Chapter 10: Home Working

More and more of us are working from home some of, or all of, the time. But rather than being a blessing this can sometimes introduce even more problems with your time management. Chapter ten looks at how you can deal with these problems and work effectively from home.

Chapter 11: Stress

Stress can make your life a misery and lead to serious illness. We look at the causes of stress, the outward signs of it and what you can do to reduce it.

Chapter 12: Life and Everything

Yes there is a life outside of work and it is vitally important if you are to live a happy and healthy life. In this chapter we look at why you should schedule these non-working activities into your life and how they will help you at work.

Chapter 13: Personal Action Plan

The final chapter outlines an approach to developing a personal action plan to take you on the next step of your journey through life. It ends with a helpful list of the top 20 tips for effective time management.

While you can 'cherry pick' any of the chapters or topics that interest you, it is worth working through the first three chapters as they set out the guidelines for developing effective time management.

If you utilize just a few of the techniques in this book you will be able to make substantial improvements in your time management. And the good news is, the more you use the better it gets.

Summary

- Time management is not about the time you spend working but about the *way* you spend your working time

- Rather than working longer and longer hours and working 'harder' we need to think about working 'smarter'

- Effective time management can result in substantial benefits to you and your organization

- Seven steps to effective time management: understand what you spend your time on now; identify what you want to achieve; develop a plan for achieving it; include time in your daily plan for things that will happen; prioritize the important tasks; review at the end of each day; and review progress at the strategic level

- We need time management to cope with the everyday challenges we face and increasing our time awareness will help us deal with them

- We can't manage time itself but we can manage the way we use the time that is available to us

- Rather than taking work home and ruining our personal time, effective time management will provide the solution

- Develop a plan to break out of the current situation and begin a happier and more successful life

- Time is difficult to define and we can't change it but it does seem to speed up when we are busy and slow down when we are not busy so we need to harness this to our advantage

- We need to identify the positive things we want to do more of and also the things we want to stop doing

- Time is not money, it is far more important than that and we should invest it wisely for our future benefit

- The first step towards effective time management is to recognise that you are the one person responsible for how you spend your time

- Once you have accepted that, you can start to define your personal objectives for what you want to get from life and what you want to get from effective time management

2 Time Flies

This chapter explores how we use our time, keeping a time log and analyzing it. It then looks at how we work and how we can change it for the better.

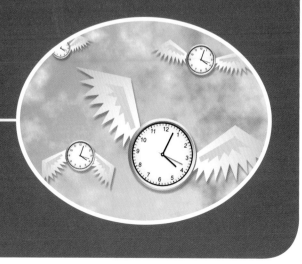

Where Time Goes

In this chapter we want to explore where all the time goes. We know it goes somewhere because there never seems to be enough of it left when we need it. Let us examine some of the common problems we all have to deal with:

Your Worst Enemy

John Adair, one of the foremost authorities on leadership, said: "Look in the mirror and you will see your biggest time waster." Until you accept that fact few, if any, of your personal time problems will be overcome. What we are talking about is:

Procrastination

Often referred to as the 'thief of time':

"Never do today what you can put off until tomorrow" (Anon).

"I like work; I could watch it for hours" (Jerome K Jerome).

Sometimes it's right to delay making a decision but usually it's better to make the decision and get on with things. The tougher or more unpleasant the decision, the more likely we are to put it off until tomorrow. So don't let procrastination take root. Just get on and do it!

Poor Delegation

We all know that delegation can save you time and it helps to develop other people. It makes your time available for the more important things you do and enriches the job of the person you are delegating to. Effective delegation is all about making the best use of everyone's time.

But watch out for upward delegation, this is where people who report to you keep escalating things to you rather than making decisions themselves!

Disorganized People

Disorganized people think they are busy but often aren't. They may well be snowed under heaps of paperwork and it's all disorganized. They end up spending all their time trying to find things or trying to remember what it was they were doing.

When they do manage to start something, they immediately get interrupted. They go home wondering if they actually achieved anything and they are probably right, they didn't!

Beware

While it is flattering to be asked to help, it is better to encourage others to help themselves.

Ineffective Meetings

I'm sure we have all attended the 'meeting from hell'. People shuffle in over a 10 minute period (including the chairperson, who promptly sets about trying to find bits of paper to remind himself or herself what the meeting was about in the first place).

Agenda, don't make me laugh! They spend the first 15 minutes chatting about some mutual friend you don't know. When the meeting does finally get around to discussing the business you came for people start getting up to leave: "sorry another meeting to go to" or "I arranged to pick the kids up" and so on!

Meetings are essential but you can help ensure they are effective by asking for an agenda and a time limit, only attending when there is a need, and ensuring that the meeting deals with things effectively.

Lack of Direction

It is very difficult to make sensible decisions about how to spend your time if you have no clear objectives or goals. Ask yourself what your 'core mission' is. What does the organization actually pay you to do? Once you know that, you also need to know the priorities, what should take precedence. Is it just the last thing your manager tells you to do or the next phone call you get? Make sure you clarify your aims and priorities in terms of importance and urgency (not always the same thing) so you know what to use your time on.

Growing Backlog

A growing backlog of work, a growing backlog of unanswered emails, and an ever-lengthening To Do list. These are all symptoms of failure to keep up with the job. The answer is not working longer hours and taking work home (which we will look at in the next topic). When you're overworked you need to work *smarter* not harder.

Hot tip

Don't try to work harder, try to work smarter.

How to Deal with These Problems

So did any of these common problems apply to you? Be honest with yourself. If they did, then make a commitment to yourself to work on them and add them to your list of objectives for improving your time management. We will be introducing techniques for dealing with all of these problems throughout the rest of the book.

Working Hours

In the previous topic we looked at where the time goes and some of the common problems we can face. Most of us deal with these problems by working longer hours, taking work home, skipping lunch and so on. If you are working more than 40 hours a week, then you are overworked.

Are You Overworked?

Be honest with yourself and work through the checklist below. For each question give it one of the following scores:

    0 you never do it

    1 you rarely do it

    2 you sometimes do it

    3 you often do it

    4 you nearly always do it

The Checklist

There are just six questions; be honest and score each of them:

1) Do you work late?

2) Do you take work home?

3) Do you skip a proper lunch break?

4) Do you feel you've too much to do?

5) Do you have to rush to meet deadlines?

6) Do you end up feeling stressed at the end of the day?

What it Means

Now add up the total of all your scores.

0-6   you should have no real worries if it stays at this level

7-12   is not too bad but be careful it doesn't get any worse

13-18   you need to take a good look at the way you work

19-24   you need to take a long, hard look at the way you work

Ask yourself why you choose to work excessive hours: Has your boss asked you to? Is it peer pressure as all your colleagues do it? Is it part of the ethos of your organization?

Home Truths

If you are dealing with the pressures of work by working more, here are a few home truths for you:

- Working a 60 hour week is not effective. It is just not possible to work 10 hours a day, 6 days a week (or any other permutation) and still be effective

- The longer you work without a break the less effective your work will become

- It is better to work fewer hours and use the time well than to work more hours and use the time badly

- Reduce the hours you work but make them more effective and your organization will benefit in that the quality of your work will be significantly better

- You will benefit as working fewer hours will mean you have a better life outside of work

- You will also benefit because you feel more effective at work and will therefore be happier

- Your organization will also benefit from these last two points as well, a win-win situation

Beware

Working excessive hours can have a serious impact on your health and wellbeing.

Overworked?

If you scored more than 12 on the checklist opposite or suffer any other problems associated with being overworked, add another objective to your list: to work fewer hours but smarter rather than working harder. The rest of this book will show you how to go about it.

Where Time Goes

To get back to the topic of where all the time goes: if you are overworked you are probably using it trying to catch up most of the time. Even if you are not overworked (which is unlikely if you are reading this) you still need to know where the time goes before you can do anything about improving your time management effectiveness.

We will look at finding out exactly what you do spend your time on over the next two topics: Keeping a Time Log, and Analyzing your Time.

27

Keeping a Time Log

The reason for keeping a time log is to learn from it, and one of the most effective forms of learning is referred to as experiential learning or learning by experience.

Experiential Learning
Experiential learning states that we learn most effectively when we go through four steps of a cyclical process:

1 Planning: define the task or activity that we are going to do and how we are going to do it

2 Experience: carry out the task or activity

3 Review: how it actually worked out compared to how we expected it to

4 Learn: from that review and draw conclusions from it to feed into planning the next experience

It doesn't matter where we start (as it is a cycle) but the learning process is most effective when we go through all four steps.

Reviewing
In order to really understand how time flies you need to start by reviewing how you currently spend your time compared to how you think you spend it. Then you can learn from it and plan to use your time more effectively in future. To be really effective you need to repeat the cycle every so often.

What Do You Spend Your Time On?
So what do you think you spend your time on and how do you know? Start by recording how you think you currently spend your time using the categories in Analyzing Your Time on page 30. But be prepared to be in for a surprise.

"Don't depend on memory, it's treacherous" (Peter Drucker).
The only way to be sure is to record it in a time log.

Developing a Time Log
You can use a desk diary or sheet of paper. You need to split the day into 15 minute segments (anything smaller will be difficult to cope with and anything larger will be too inaccurate).

Hot tip

This cyclical learning process really does reinforce the learning experience.

Beware

Don't assume you know what you spend your time on, you will find you are wrong!

① As you work through the day, record each task or activity that you work on as you start it and end it

② Use codes to make it easy (there are some suggested ones in the next topic on the following page)

③ Review your time log at the end of each day, filling in anything in that you missed

④ Summarize it at the end of each week (you will need to run it for at least two weeks)

The following is an example of part of a daily time log:

TIME LOG	Monday	
Time	Activity	Comments
08:00	P	Coffee & review day plan
08:15	R	Check emails & reply
08:30		
08:45	J	Walk floor & greet staff
09:00	M	Stand Up Meeting
09:15		
09:30	D	Jim Biggs schedule
09:45		
10:00	T	Joe Brown visit plan
10:15		
10:30		Coffee
10:45	W	Monthly report
11:00	W	
11:15	C	Costing for report
11:30	T	Mary Jones training
11:45	W	Monthly report
12:00	W	
12:15		Grab sandwich
12:45	W	Monthly report
13:00	T	Boss needs sales figures
13:15	C	Sales figures
Etc...		

Analyzing your Time

In the previous topic we saw why we need to record our time and how to keep it simple. The easiest way is to use a set of codes to describe each activity rather than having to write in the detail.

Activity Codes
The weekly summary sheet below contains a suggested list of possible activity codes. Please adapt and add to it to suit the activities in your job.

Daily Review
Review your time log at the end of the day and complete it by filling in any missing gaps. If you leave it to tomorrow you will have forgotten the detail.

Summarize
At the end of each week summarize what you spent your time on, review it and reflect on how you actually spend your time in comparison to what you thought you would spend your time on.

Hot tip

Review your day plan at the start of each day and your time log at the end of it. Then compare them.

Weekly Summary

	Total Hours	Percentage
M=Meetings	5	11%
D=Discussions	7	16%
E=Education/training	3	7%
P=Telephone	8	18%
C=Calculations	2	5%
W=Writing/word processing	5	11%
R=Reading (paper/e-mail/etc)	8	18%
J=Walking the job	1	2%
T=Travel	3	7%
P=Planning/thinking	2	5%
O=Other (specify)		
Weekly Total:	44	100%

Reflect

Now that you have the actual details of how you spent your time for one week you can ask yourself some questions:

1. How did the percentages of your time spent on the various activities compare to what you were expecting?

2. Did you spend the bulk of your time on your core responsibilities and, if not, why not?

3. Is there anything that you spent time on that did nothing to contribute to your role?

4. If so, what would happen if you just stopped doing it?

5. How much of your time was available for you to use as you wished, rather than being dictated by other people?

6. Could this be consolidated into one or two larger chunks rather than split into small segments?

7. Could you have done any of the work faster or simpler without adversely affecting anyone else?

8. Could you have delegated anything, particularly repetitive tasks to someone else?

Learn From It

Now that you have reflected on what actually happened, compared to what you expected to happen, what can you learn from it? You should be able to identify activities that consume a significant amount of your time without a commensurate benefit. These should be flagged for reduction or removal.

You should also be able to identify activities that are core or critical to your job that you should be spending more time on. There may even be activities that you should have spent time on but weren't able to. All of this learning should then be fed into your planning process for the next week.

How We Work

John Adair produced the following composite picture from over 20 studies and observations of managers:

Working Hours

They work long hours including taking work home and attending business meetings and social events connected with their work. They can end up dealing with hundreds of different things in a single day. This seemed to apply mostly to management and not to apply to people in well-defined roles such as accountants.

Fragmentation

Their work is typically fragmented into brief periods of two to nine minute chunks. The chunks of work are not done in any particular sequence.

Priority

They make no attempt to assess the priority or urgency of anything. Everything is effectively treated as urgent and problems and issues are dealt with reactively as they occur.

Interruptions

They are continually interrupted by telephone calls and visitors. One manager received 40 phone calls and 30 visitors in a single day. Their other work has to take place interspersed with these intrusions.

Location

Most of their work is done in their own offices or in their department. Very little time is spent by Western senior managers on the 'shop floor', which is in complete contrast to the practice of senior managers in Japan.

Planning

Few managers are skilled planners and they are unlikely to have clear periods of time which they can devote to this key activity. They spend less than 5% of their time on it.

Estimation

Managers are not good at estimating how much time they spend on the various activities they perform. They tend to overestimate the time they spend on production, paperwork, telephone and thinking. They underestimate the time they spend in meetings and discussions.

Hot tip

Once you start recording your time, your estimates should get much better.

Time Management

They have very little control over how they spend their time and seem to be totally event-driven and reactive.

Conclusions

There are a number of conclusions that can be drawn from the results of this study:

1. We should start by acknowledging that we do not know how we spend our time and any assumptions we might have are probably wrong

2. In order to start from a factual baseline, we need to observe how we spend our time in detail and record it for at least one and preferably two weeks

3. Having recorded our time in detail we should then summarize it at the end of each week and analyze how we actually spent it

4. We then need to compare it to how we thought we spent our time and how we should be spending it, in line with our job description or priorities

5. Then we can identify the specific actions we will take to improve how we spend it

These results would seem to reinforce the previous topic and underlie the importance of understanding how we really do spend our time.

Summary

It would seem that most of us mismanage our time. Until you learn to manage your use of time you will not be able to manage anything else. What you need to do is develop your own personal time awareness so that you become conscious of how you are spending or wasting the precious time that is available to you.

Once you have this awareness you are ready to move on to the next step, which is changing the way you work. This process is dealt with in the next topic.

Beware

If you don't plan your time you will never be in control of it.

Don't forget

If you don't know how you spend your time now, you will never be able to improve it.

33

Changing It

What we need to do is change our approach to work so that we can do more of the things that matter and fewer of the things that don't. If you've gone through the process of recording your time accurately in some form of time log and analyzing how you spent your time at the end of each week, you should have a list of the things you need to change. If you haven't yet done that take a look at two of the earlier topics: Where Time Goes (page 24) and How We Work (page 32) for some potential bad working habits that might apply to you.

Time Awareness

The first thing you need to change is your time awareness. The time log and analysis should have started this process. You now need to commit to staying aware of how you are spending your time. Reinforce this from time to time by repeating the time log for a week. This lays the foundations for everything else.

Eliminate Bad Habits

If you suffer from any of the problems listed earlier then add it to the list of things you are going to change. Advice on how to change most of them are covered by chapters or topics later in this book.

Stop Procrastinating

If you suffer from this you really do have to make a commitment to yourself to stop wasting time. When faced with a difficult decision, ask yourself if you are capable of making the decision. If you are, then make it; if not escalate it to someone who can. But beware, every time you do this you are asking someone else to make a decision for you. This is at least better than just hoping the problem will go away.

Get Organized

We have a whole chapter (chapter five) on this later but the first step is to commit to sorting yourself out. That means organizing your desk, your workspace and how you spend your day.

Improved Planning

The only way you will eliminate bad practices and focus on what really matters is by planning. Again there is a whole chapter (chapter three) on this vital subject but make a start today by identifying the things you should be doing and scheduling them into you diary first. When you've done that stick to it.

Hot tip

There is a topic on effective decision making on page 104.

34

Stop Working Excessive Hours

Get a life, as the saying goes. Commit to limiting the hours you work to a reasonable level so that you can enjoy life outside work. You may not be able to change this overnight but you should be able to reduce it gradually. Start by leaving work at a reasonable time one day a week and then gradually increase it.

Eliminate Time Wasting

As part of developing your time awareness, you need to identify the time wasting activities that you get involved in and cut them out. Do you really need to go to every meeting you are invited to? Do you need to stay for the whole meeting if there is only one topic that involves you? Before you schedule any activity ask yourself if you really need to do it. Before you say yes to any request, think if it is something you really should be doing, which leads nicely onto the next topic.

Learn to Say No

You can say no and you can do it without being unpleasant or upsetting other people (this is covered in detail in chapter six). So make a commitment to yourself that you will say no, so that you stop over-committing yourself.

Make Meetings Effective

If you must have a meeting then at least ensure it makes the best use of everyone's time. This applies to your own meetings and any other people's that you attend. Chapter eight is full of help and advice on this subject.

Reduce Stress

If you currently suffer from stress there is no point telling yourself to stop being stressed, it will only make things worse. Learn to reduce stress by eliminating the things that cause it and by taking more exercise, relaxing and making better use of your free time. Chapter eleven covers this in depth.

Start Enjoying Life

Make a commitment to start enjoying life. Schedule things into your life that you enjoy, outside work, with your friends, family and loved ones. Take up a new hobby or sport. But work can be fun too, what about arranging an event or outing with colleagues? Start enjoying life and spread goodwill and happiness to others as well as to yourself.

Hot tip

The more effectively you manage your time the more enjoyable life will become.

Summary

- Common time problems are procrastination, poor delegation, disorganized management, ineffective meetings, lack of direction and a growing backlog of work

- Working a 60 hour week is not effective; the longer we work the more our work deteriorates. It's better to work fewer hours and use them well than more hours and use them badly

- The most effective learning process is when you go through a cyclical process of planning an activity, carrying it out, reviewing how it worked and learning from it for when you plan the next activity

- Do not assume you know how you spend your time, so record it in detail for at least one week, if not two, in a time log

- At the end of each week summarize and analyze your time log, reflect on how it compared to your expectations and learn from that for your next plan

- Studies of working managers have found that they worked long hours, work was fragmented into small chunks, they did not prioritize the work, they were continually interrupted, they did not plan effectively, they were poor at estimating work and had little control over how they spent their time

- Most of us mismanage our time and, unless you can learn to manage how you spend your time, you will not be able to manage anything else

- Make a committed approach to improving your time awareness as, without this, you will not be able to identify the things you need to change

- You then need to identify your bad habits and work on eliminating them

- Avoid procrastination, get yourself properly organized and start planning

- Make a commitment to stop working excessive hours, eliminate any time-wasting activities, learn how to say no, make meetings more effective, reduce stress and begin to enjoy life, both in and outside of work

3 Priorities

Sorting out the priorities of your work is vital if you are to manage your time effectively. This chapter covers prioritizing work and planning it.

How Time Gets Used

In chapter two we identified how we currently use our time, now we can move on to thinking about how we want to spend it. We can split the way our time gets used into four basic categories: dealing with crises and problems that are thrust on us; the demands of other people; things we do out of sheer habit and planned prioritized work. Let us look at each of them.

Crises and Problems

Some people find it exciting to go from one near-catastrophe to the next by fixing broken hardware or software, dealing with angry customers, finding replacements when someone is suddenly off sick and resolving conflicts. Crises will always happen but by establishing how much time should be spent in different areas and better planning and delegation we should be able to reduce the time we spend on crisis management.

Demands of Others

Our bosses, colleagues, customers, sales departments, friends and families all place demands on our time. If we try to satisfy them all we become stressed and lose sight of what we are really trying to achieve. We need to rationalize these demands.

Habit

We all do things out of habit or routine behavior that we don't even think about. We just do some things because we always have done. We need to make sure we only do things that are beneficial and not a hindrance to our effectiveness.

Planned and Prioritized Work

When we plan and prioritize our work we are making decisions about how we spend our time. These are the things that are the most important to us in the performance of our jobs. And yet we often find that the first three categories take precedence over this critical category of our work.

How Do You Use Your Time?

What percentage of your work time would you say you actually spend on each of these four categories? Work it out on a piece of paper and make sure the four add up to 100%.

Would you be more effective if you changed the percentages?

What percentage do you think you should spend on each?

How We Should Use Our Time

Learning to manage your time more effectively means you can decide to spend time on the right things and learn to say no or limit the time you spend on the other categories. Use the following steps:

1 Make sure that your planned and prioritized work is given top priority by scheduling it into your day plan

2 Then deal with any crises or problems that occur by delegating the action to someone else or dealing with it when you have some free time after completing your planned and prioritized work

This may sound harsh but in practice many crises and problems go away of their own accord in time. The person bringing you the problem may find they can fix it themselves rather that wait for you, which produces a win-win situation.

3 Consider the demands of others when they come up, but recognize that you will not have enough time to deal with them all. Filter them out by relegating them to a lower order of priority

Then you can deal with them only when and if you have the free time available. If not, you need to consider what else you can do with them, such as delegation or plain refusal.

4 Finally consider the things you do out of sheer habit and ask yourself if they have any business benefit or are a valuable use of your time and if not, drop them

If any of the things you do from habit do have a business value, then they should be part of your planned prioritized work and scheduled (as in step one above). If not, then you should stop yourself from doing them.

The Way Forward

To change the percentage of your time that you spend on each of these categories you need to plan it. Which takes us nicely on to the next topic.

Hot tip

Prioritize work using these four steps and you will always be more effective.

Planning

If you are going to change the amount of time that you spend on the different types of activity, then you need to plan it. Planning is one of, if not the most critical of the business skills. It is often said that an hour spent in planning a task will save approximately three hours' work in carrying it out. So time spent in planning is time well spent.

Broadly speaking there are three types of plan and to be effective you need to develop them in sequence:

Long Term Plans

Strategic plans, as they are sometimes called, are the long term plans which focus on your strategic goals or objectives. These should answer questions such as: where do I want to be in five years' time and what am I going to do to move towards achieving that goal?

Some people suggest you should plan out your whole life but that is not very realistic as so many things are likely to happen along the way. Five years is an effective period for a long term plan and, even in that time frame, you are likely to need to make some significant changes to your plan.

Mid Term Plans

Having defined where you want to get to, the operational or mid-term plans define what you want to do over the next six to twelve months to help achieve it. These will normally be aligned to your job plans and review periods (hence the six to twelve month time-frame). But the plans need to be reviewed more frequently to check you are on track and, if necessary, take corrective actions.

Short Term Plans

Some time management specialists suggest planning a week or even a month ahead. But even if you do that, you will still need to get down to a tactical or day plan to define what you are going to do today to be effective.

All three of these plans need to be in place if you are going to manage your time effectively. The long term plan defines your strategic direction. The mid term plan sets out what you are going to do to move towards achieving it over the next year. The short term plan defines what you are going to do to towards achieving it today.

Long Term Plans

Strategic plans about our career and life goals

Typically over a five year horizon

Medium Term Plans

Operational plans about what we want
to achieve in the job and our personal
development plans

Typically over a one year horizon

Short Term

What we plan to
do today

Long Term Plans

These are your long term strategic goals or objectives. They should answer the questions about what you want to do with your life and where you want to be in five years' time.

Life can be compared to a journey and the long term plan is a road map for that journey with some directions and milestones. Then you can check from time to time if you are still heading in the right direction or even if your goals have changed.

Creating The Plan

Use the template opposite to create your long term plan following these five steps:

1. First of all, you need to understand your values, the things that really matter to you in life, and list these at the top of the form

2. Then summarize what you are heading towards, what you want to be doing in five years' time (or a longer or shorter time frame if more appropriate)

3. Then you can start to identify the things you want to do and achieve; they can be business, personal, sporting or even political ambitions

4. Remember that a good objective should be SMART: Strategic, Measurable, Agreed, Realistic and Timed

5. Once you have listed all your strategic objectives, prioritize them so that the most important are at the top and the least important at the bottom

This long term plan should be for your own personal use and need not be shared with your organization or boss unless you want to share it. A good boss should ask you what your strategic objectives are anyway and a bad one will probably not be interested.

Once you've created your long term plan, you can move on to creating your mid term or operational plan. This will identify what you want to achieve towards your long term objectives over the next year.

Strategic Objectives

Write down the values that matter to you in life

Where you want to be in five years' time

List your strategic objectives in priority order

1.

2.

3.

4.

5.

6.

7.

Hot tip

Once you have created your long term objectives take time to review them at least once a year.

Mid Term Plans

These mid term or operational plans should cover the current review period. Typically they will be one year but they could be shorter if you are working in a rapidly changing environment. These may be the things that feature in your current job plan, as that is exactly what a job plan is.

Job Responsibilities

Peter Drucker once said that you should ask yourself if you know what you are being paid to do. What are the two or three things, which if you perform them well, will make a real difference? Your mid term operational plan should answer this question.

Your objectives should map onto your job responsibilities. These are the things you are being paid to do. There should also be an indication of the percentage of your time that you should be spending on each responsibility.

Objectives

Starting from your long term objectives, ask yourself what you need to achieve to move towards them. This should give you your key goals or objectives for the next year. What should be different in a year's time? In order to do this you will need to stand back from the day-to-day detail and look at the broader picture. For each objective ask yourself what you will have to do to achieve it and list these steps. Each is effectively a sub-objective.

Things to Stop Doing

Using the results of the time log and analysis from chapter two and the results from how time gets used in this chapter, identify the things that you want to spend less time on. Ask yourself if you can stop doing them, delegate them to someone else or change the way that you do them to be more effective.

Once you are satisfied that you have a suitable mid term plan, share it with your boss. In a good organization and with a good boss they would probably have asked you to do this anyway.

Planning

A good plan should answer a number of questions: who, what, when, where, why and how.

Time spent in planning can actually save time in implementation. Just getting on and doing it usually means having to sort things out as you go along while planning first means you can be much more focused on the implementation.

Creating the Plan

Start with your existing mid term plan if you have one, or what you think it should be if you don't:

1 List all of your prioritized objectives for the coming year

2 Identify the approximate percentage of your time that should be spent on each

3 Then add the target date for achieving each or for reviewing it if it won't be completed in the current planning period

4 Next list your training and development needs and what you need from the organization to help you achieve your objectives

5 Then list any support needs, the things you need from your manager or colleagues to help you achieve your objectives

6 Finally add the date for the next review of your progress towards meeting the plan

This plan should determine your work priorities and it should be shared with your manager as part of your job review and planning process.

Review

These operational plans need to be reviewed about once a quarter, either with your manager or by yourself. Ask what you have achieved and what you have failed to achieve and why. Then ask yourself if the plan needs to be revised in any way in light of this or if you need to change some of the things you are doing.

Once you have established your mid term operational plan, you can move on to short term planning.

Short Term Plans

Our short term or tactical plans set out how we intend to use the time that is immediately available to us. Today is a natural, understandable and very planable unit of time.

Day Plan

In developing your day plan, a diary or some form of day planner is an excellent starting point. Review your time management objectives and mid range plan, as your day plan should be structured around these objectives. Then develop your day plan using the following steps:

1. Schedule in any meetings as blocks of time, including the time for any preparation, getting to the meeting, getting back and writing up any notes or actions following the meeting

2. Schedule in one or more blocks of time for reading and responding to emails and paper mail

3. Schedule in blocks of time for any major activities such as planning, report writing, calculations, etc.

4. Schedule in a lunch break and at least one morning and afternoon break

5. Schedule in one or more blocks of time for dealing with important tasks

At this stage you may or may not have any free time left in the day. If you have, then keep it free, don't be tempted to schedule every minute, as you will be able to use it if it really is available.

There is an example day plan opposite, which shows the scheduled blocks of time shaded in light red and the remaining free time shaded in light green.

What we have done in creating our day plan is schedule how we want to use our time. This should look very similar to the time log we created when we were recording how we spent out time. The day plan is an aspiration of how we want to use our time and the time log is a record of the actual time we spent.

Day Plan

08:00   Review & finalize day plan
Check mail and emails and reply

09:00   Project Team Stand Up Meeting
Write up actions and notes

10:00   Jim Biggs: review of schedule

Coffee

11:00   Joe Brown: discuss travel plans

12:00   Monthly Report

13:00   Lunch with Gill & Jim

14:00   Important Tasks (see Action List)

15:00

16:00   Check emails and phone messages and reply
Finish Monthly Report

17:00   Jog in the park with Bill

18:00

Action List

The Action List (or To Do List) is a record of all the tasks that you have identified you need to do. In its simplest form it will just be a list of tasks. Typically you will tend to work through the action list in one of three ways:

● Starting at the top and working your way down: but the problem with this is that you are usually adding tasks to the bottom faster than you are crossing them off the top

● Dealing with the tasks that are the most urgent first: but the problem with this is that all tasks end up becoming urgent if you put off doing them

● Dealing with the quick or easy tasks first: this means you can cross some off, but that risks urgent tasks being late

Creating the Action List

There has to be a better way and there is. By making the action list a bit more sophisticated you can prioritize the most important tasks, the ones that really matter to the business:

1 List all the tasks that you have to do on your action list

2 Note alongside each task when they are due to be completed or when you want to have done them by

3 Based on this decide how urgent each task is

4 Decide how important each task is to the business

Urgent or Important?

These last two things are not the same. You can easily find that you spend a lot of time dealing with urgent but not necessarily important tasks, rather than tackling the important tasks that are central to your role and will help you achieve your objectives.

The grid at the top of the page opposite illustrates tasks graded into four categories based on their urgency and importance.

A tasks are both urgent and important. These must be given the top priority but the danger is that you won't allocate (or be able to give) enough time to them.

Urgent or Important

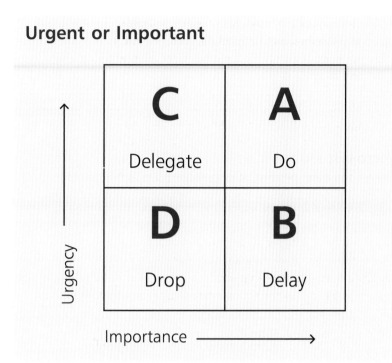

B tasks are important but not (yet) urgent. They should be your second priority but only after the A tasks are complete.

C tasks are urgent but not important. Don't even look at them until the A and B tasks are complete.

D tasks (often simple or easy tasks which are therefore attractive to do) should not be done at all.

On this basis A tasks will always get done, B tasks will usually get done, C tasks might not get done (unless or until they become A tasks), and D tasks will never get done unless or until they become important to the business:

1 Schedule A tasks into your day plan/diary

2 If you have some spare time left after you've done them, then do some B tasks

3 Consider delegating C tasks and dropping D tasks altogether

Beware

D tasks are where we go to escape when work becomes too much, don't do it!

Organizers

In developing a short term plan we mentioned using a diary or organizer. While many people still prefer to use a desk diary with a day per page to keep track of their schedule, time log and notes, more and more of us are turning to electronic organizers. Portable devices can now synchronize automatically with a desktop computer organizer which means we can take our day plan with us wherever we go.

Microsoft Outlook

One of the most popular desktop organizers is Microsoft Outlook, which provides tools for tracking appointments and tasks as well as contacts and email. The following illustration shows a day plan with A priority tasks:

In the illustration above different colors have been used to differentiate the various types of activity in place of activity codes. Tasks at their due date are listed in the task panel as a reminder to schedule them in to the day plan.

Other Organizers

There are other desktop computer organizers which provide similar functions to Microsoft Outlook. There are also loose-leaf folder organizers such as Time Manager and Filofax, wall charts and of course portable electronic devices. All have their benefits and potential disadvantages.

IBM Lotus Organizer

Very similar in functionality to Microsoft Outlook, Lotus Organizer has integrated functions for: calendar, contact management, To Do lists, web access, scheduling and many others. Its strong points are its sophisticated printing facilities and drag and drop between the web and other applications.

Time Manager

Like Filofax and other hard copy time managers, Time Manager provides a time management system. This covers a loose-leaf binder in various size options, back up filing and a range of section dividers and refill packs for the calendar and other sections. Its strong point is that it is hard copy but that is also its disadvantage.

Planning Charts

Wall charts are still popular with teams so they can track one another's activities and whereabouts. There is a huge range of preprinted charts available and there are even free charts that can be downloaded from the internet and printed.

Electronic Organizers

Electronic organizers or personal digital assistants (PDAs) bring together the features of the desktop computer organizer with the portability of a mobile phone. In fact the distinction between a PDA and mobile phone is getting very blurred.

The RIM BlackBerry pushed back the initial frontiers, and developments such as the iPhone and iPad have continued this advance.

Synchronization

The key benefit of these devices is their ability to synchronize, in both directions, with a desktop computer organizer. This not only means that both devices are up-to-date but provides a secure backup in case the handheld device is lost.

Hot tip

Whatever you are using, get into the habit of backing up all of your data regularly.

Summary

- We tend to spend our time dealing with crises, the demands of others, things we do out of habit and finally planned prioritized work

- To be effective you should aim to spend your time on planned prioritized work first, then deal with any crises, problems and the demands of others if time allows

- Don't spend time on anything out of habit; it should either be planned and prioritized if it has a business benefit or, if not, you should drop it

- To be effective you need to start with a long term plan, then develop a mid term plan which takes you in the right direction and finally produce a daily plan to prioritize the effective use of your time

- Long term plans should define what you want to do and where you want to be in five years' time, focusing on your core values and listing your strategic objectives

- Mid term plans should look forward, listing your prioritized objectives for the year, with the amount of time you should spend on each of them and any target dates for their achievement or review

- Short term or day plans should allocate blocks of time for all the things you want to do including spending time on important tasks

- Action (or To Do) lists should record all the tasks you have identified and they should be prioritized according to whether they are urgent and/or important. Only important tasks should be scheduled into your day plan

- There are a number of organizers that can help with your day plans and action lists, including Microsoft Outlook and other desktop computer organizers, loose-leaf folders, wall charts and personal digital assistants (PDAs)

- The ability of PDAs to synchronize with a desktop computer organizer provides a powerful combination of a portable day plan and action list with the security of safe back up

4 More on Time

This chapter explores some additional ways in which we can identify opportunities for using our time more effectively.

Quality Time

John Adair stated very succinctly that "The quality of time matters more than the quantity of time". It therefore stands to reason that we should make the best use of our quality time, but what exactly is our quality time?

Energy and Alertness

Our energy levels and alertness are not constants. They tend to rise and fall cyclically during the course of the day. Sometimes we feel active and raring to go and at other times we could easily nod off to sleep. Have you ever found yourself doing this at a meeting or seminar after lunch? They don't call that time period the 'graveyard slot' for nothing!

When to Use It

It clearly makes sense for us to use the times when we are most mentally active, our high quality time, for the important tasks that can benefit from it rather than waste it on low importance activities. Conversely we should try and schedule low importance activities for the times when we are not at our most alert.

When is It?

When is our high quality time? The answer is it varies from person to person but you should be able to work out when yours is by keeping a record for a few days of how you are feeling at set times over the course of the day from when you wake up in the morning to when you go to sleep at night.

For a large number of people it will be in the morning. For some people it will be the evening and, for a minority, noon or the afternoon. Whenever it is, identify it then you can plan to use it most effectively.

Scheduling

You can make the most of your quality time if you schedule important tasks that require concentration, creativity and hard work during the four or five hours when you are at your best. Conversely you should schedule interesting, social-type (less important) activities such as meetings for when you are at your least alert, as it will give you some extra stimulus.

Obviously you can't always determine when something must happen, particularly if it's not something that you are arranging. But you can often have an input to the decision.

Hot tip

If a meeting is important to you, try to get it scheduled for your quality time period.

Your Quality Time

To identify and exploit your quality time use the following steps:

1 Keep a daily record for one working week recording how alert you feel when you first wake up and then every three hours until you go to bed at night

2 Plot each day's results onto the same chart to form a composite view, as in the illustration below

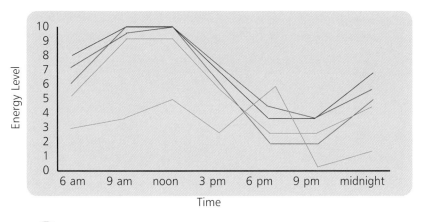

3 Remove any outliers (extreme results) such as the green day in the illustration above

4 The composite view should give a good indication of your daily time profile

In the illustration above the quality time is between 9 am and 12 noon, with the early morning 6 am to 9 am being the next best time (while energy and alertness are increasing). Conversely the afternoon should be used for less important activities.

Creative Moments

During this quality time period you are at your most creative and will sometimes come up with solutions to problems that you hadn't even been working on. This is a result of your subconscious mind continuing to work on something after you have stopped consciously working on it and we will be exploring it in the next topic, Creative Thinking.

Creative Thinking

There are as many views on creative thinking on the Web as there are for time management. What we really mean by creative thinking is being able to come up with good ideas to solve a problem or need, particularly as epitomized by thinkers such as Edward de Bono and his 'thinking outside the box'. But there are a number of problems or stumbling blocks.

Stumbling Blocks

Brian Clark of Copyblogger Media came up with this list of potential problem areas:

- Trying to find The Right Answer: when in real life there is often more than one right answer

- Logical Thinking: when real life is often illogical and logical thinking may prevent truly innovative thoughts

- Following Rules: when creative thinking is all about tearing up rules and not doing things because "everyone does them"

- Being Practical: while practicality is important, when it comes to execution it can stifle innovative ideas

- Play is Not Work: but allowing your mind to be at play can be the most effective way to stimulate creative thinking

- That's Not My Job: but it's those who happily explore completely unrelated areas of life and knowledge who find the best solution

- Being a Serious Person: leaders from Egyptian pharaohs to Chinese emperors have consulted with court jesters when faced with tough problems. Give yourself permission to be a fool and see things for what they really are

- Avoiding Ambiguity: when most situations are ambiguous and ambiguity is your friend if you're looking to innovate

- Being Wrong is Bad: we hate being wrong but making mistakes often teaches us the most

- I'm Not Creative: but we are all limitlessly creative, as long as we realize that we create our own limits

Hot tip

Believe in yourself and your creative potential, it is not limited.

So learn to recognize these stumbling blocks and overcome them by positive creative thinking

Unleash Your Subconscious

Another excellent suggestion from John Adair and others is that when faced with a mental blockage to a problem we are trying to resolve, we should put the problem aside for a while and leave our subconscious to carry on thinking for us. There are four steps to this process:

1 Preparation: the fact-gathering stage where you gather the information, analyze the problem and explore some possible solutions

2 Incubation: having completed the preparation, you move on to something else, your subconscious mind will continue to work on the problem and possibly incorporate other facts and knowledge

3 Insight: eventually these new ideas will emerge from your subconscious into your conscious mind, either slowly or sometimes as a flash of inspiration

4 Validation: then you can use your conscious mind again to test out the soundness of the ideas before taking any actions on them

So if you are using your quality time to think about a problem and nothing happens, stop and move onto something else. Your subconscious mind will carry on working on it for you.

Incubation

Incubation is therefore a temporary break from the creative problem-solving process that can result in insight into the problem. If we don't allow for this incubation period it could result in our becoming too fixated on the wrong strategy for solving the problem.

Divergent Thinking

Some researchers have also drawn a distinction between what they term convergent and divergent thinking. Convergent thinking aims for the one correct solution to a problem. Divergent thinking involves creative generation of multiple answers to the problem. See the first stumbling block opposite.

Hot tip

Sleeping on an idea is another popular way of allowing ideas to incubate before a final decision is made.

Moonlighting

John Adair coined the phrase 'moonlighting' to describe a process of using the times when you find yourself awake at night with your mind active. That might be an effective way of using the time but insomnia is a serious problem for some people. It is also one of the signs of stress, see chapter 11, but for now let us look at insomnia.

Insomnia

Self Help Magazine originally published these 15 proven tips for insomnia back in 1998 and updated them again a couple of years ago:

- Retinal Stimulation: go outside and stimulate your eyes for about 15 minutes a day with sunlight (but don't look straight into the sun)

- Avoid Taking Naps during the day as your body may not be as tired as necessary to get to sleep at night

- Keep Cool: the temperature in your bedroom should be cool and comfortable

- Waking Activities: don't watch TV, eat, talk on the telephone, text your friends or use your laptop. However, reading in bed is different as it can help you get to sleep, especially if what you are reading is boring

- Regular Bedtime: most experts agree that it is helpful to go to bed at a regular, planned time every night

- Don't Exercise within three hours of going to bed as it raises the heart rate. Slow stretching on the other hand might be just what the doctor ordered

- Don't Eat Stimulating Foods within three hours of going to bed. Lying horizontally interrupts digestion and may cause heartburn

- Avoid Stimulants such as cigarettes and caffeine (coffee, tea, cola and even some aspirin or other headache remedies can contain caffeine)

- Avoid Liquids within two hours of going to bed as liquids create the need to urinate that can awaken us and then we may not be able to get back to sleep

- Wind Down 90 minutes before you go to bed and don't do anything that might induce anxiety like checking your email or even watching the evening news

- Write Down Your Concerns: by spending a few minutes before bed at night writing down your concerns, stresses, hopes or even things you're thankful for, you can give your mind a rest while sleeping

- Calm Music/Self Hypnosis: listen to calming music, white noise, or a self-hypnosis tape for sleep. These tapes, if well produced, are scientifically designed to help you reset your brain and calm down

- Get Up: if you can't fall asleep after 15-20 minutes get up out of bed and move about

- Avoid Bright Lights: if you wake up in the middle of the night and can't get back to sleep within 30 minutes, get up but avoid as much light as possible

- Redirect Nightmares or Bad Thoughts: by focusing on a different ending. Write down your nightmare or concern, as it helps to stop the continual thoughts

Many of these suggestions make a lot of sense if we think about them but some of them are phrased in a negative way using words such as "Don't" or "Avoid". If you are going to try implementing any of them, it might be better to phrase them in a positive way such as "I will exercise in the early evening" or "I will keep a dim night-light in the bedroom".

Two of the suggestions involve writing down concerns or bad thoughts, which brings us back to Moonlighting.

Moonlighting

John Adair suggests we keep a note pad and pen by the side of the bed and jot down anything that occurs to us or is troubling us and keeps us awake during the night. The act of writing it down should help to clear our mind and help us get back to sleep.

That is very much in line with the proven tips and as an added bonus you will have your notes to remind you or trigger your creative thinking in the morning.

Don't forget

Insomnia can just be a symptom of another problem, such as stress, so ask yourself what is causing it.

Beware

Negative resolutions 'to stop doing something' are not as effective as positive resolutions.

The Pareto Principle

The Italian economist Vilfredo Pareto (1848-1923) created a mathematical formula describing the unequal distribution of wealth in his country. He observed that around 20% of the people owned 80% of the wealth. This was later taken on by others and eventually became known as Pareto's Principle or the 80/20 Rule.

The 80/20 Rule

The 80/20 Rule states that, in anything, the few (20%) are vital and the many (80%) are trivial. This is based on the mathematical probability that if a resource is shared among a sufficiently large set of participants, there must be a number, k, between 50 and 100, such that k% is taken by (100–k)% of the participants. The number k may vary from 50 in the case of equal distribution (i.e. all of the participants have equal shares) to nearly 100 (when a tiny number of participants account for almost all of the resource). There is nothing special about the 80% mathematically, but many real systems have k somewhere around this region of imbalance in distribution.

The 80/20 Rule can be applied to almost anything, from application development to time management and many other fields in between. Some commonly-cited examples are:

- 80% of your profits come from 20% of your customers

- 80% of your complaints come from 20% of your customers

- 80% of your profits come from 20% of the time you spend

- 80% of your sales come from 20% of your products

- 80% of your sales are made by 20% of your sales staff

- 80% of health care resources are used by 20% of patients

- 80% of crimes are committed by 20% of criminals

There are probably many more. In the financial services industry the concept is known as profit risk, where 20% of a company's customers are generating positive income, while 80% are costing the company money.

Microsoft noted that by fixing the top 20% of the most reported bugs, 80% of the errors and crashes were eliminated.

The Pareto principle formed a prominent part of "The 4 Hour

Workweek" by Tim Ferriss. Ferriss recommended focusing our attention on the 20% of our customers who contribute 80% of the profit. More dramatically, he also recommended firing (refusing to do business with) the 20% of customers who take up the majority of our time and cause the most trouble.

Many businesses have made dramatic improvements in their profitability by focusing on the most effective areas of their business and eliminating, ignoring, automating, delegating or retraining the rest, as appropriate.

By combining the focus on profitable customers and the effective areas of our business we can make dramatic improvements in the profitability of our business, albeit with an initial potential reduction in our sales turnover. But as the well-known saying goes, "Turnover is vanity, profit is sanity".

How It Can Help

The value of the Pareto Principle is that it reminds us to focus on the 20% of everything that matters, the things which are important to the business. Of the things we do during our normal day, only 20% really matter. But that 20% of our effort produces 80% of our results as long as we identify and focus on the things that really do matter to the business.

When the crises and problems of the day occur, as they inevitably will, and they begin to eat into our time, we need to remind ourselves of the 20% we should be focusing on. If something has to slip or if something isn't going to get done so that we can deal with the crisis, we need to make sure it's not part of that 20%.

Don't drop the important tasks, drop a non-critical meeting. The fact that you are dealing with a crisis is sufficient reason and if you ask the chairperson, they will always send you the minutes or give you a brief synopsis. So the message is don't work harder, work smarter on the right things.

Quality Time

Getting back to the principle of quality time, the Pareto Principle also applies to this. 80% of our creative work will be done in 20% of our time. This should predominantly be our quality time, the four or so hours when we are at our best.

61

Hot tip

The Pareto Principle can be applied to nearly every aspect of business.

Spare Time

We often find ourselves waiting idly for something to happen. It could be waiting for a bus, train or plane. It could be waiting for someone we have an appointment with. It could be sitting in the doctor's or dentist's waiting room. This time is spare time and it can all be put to good use along with other spare time.

Routine Time

The time we spend doing very routine things can often be used for other thinking-type activities as well. Walking, cycling, regular daily exercise, washing the dishes, cleaning or mowing the lawn; these are all activities where your brain may be in neutral.

This gives you an ideal opportunity to think about other things. If you have a prioritized action list think about the top few items and see if you can come up with any inspiration. Think back over anything you put on the back burner, waiting some free time, well that time is now. If it happens to be in your quality time zone, your subconscious may even have something ready to deliver to your conscious mind.

Waiting Time

The time we spend sitting about waiting for a bus, train, plane or a person. Waiting in airports always seems to be the most frustrating as you have to hang on in there in case there is an announcement about your flight. If you're with a companion you can get a break but if you're on your own it's not so easy.

If you have your action list, you can often fit a number of short tasks easily into what would otherwise be idle waiting time. Write a short letter, plan your next day or prepare some notes on an issue or problem. All these types of activity can use time which would otherwise be totally wasted.

Travel Time

The plane, train or bus finally departs, which now leaves you in a seat for sometimes quite long periods of time. You could read the in-flight magazine, watch an old movie or TV program, do some SuDoku puzzles or do something more creative.

The good news is that you are not in your office so you can't be disturbed. This is an ideal time for turning to important tasks that require some thought. If you have a mobile phone turn it off while you are working, you can always pick up your messages later.

Car Travel

Travel by car is the exception here as, if you are driving, you must clearly concentrate on that task. Unfortunately driving yourself is a waste of time, but sometimes you have to do it. Don't be tempted to have your mobile phone on hands-free, it's not recommended for road safety purposes.

What you can do while driving is listen to things. This is probably one very practical use for educational or foreign language disks. Again you may have recorded something that you would like to listen to when you have the time; well this could be that time.

Television

Packaged entertainment is a real waster of time. The average American and European now watches eight hours or more of television entertainment per day. They also see an awful lot of commercials encouraging them to buy things. An ever growing proportion of the population is becoming obese and/or is now classed as semi-illiterate. Television has a lot to answer for!

If you want to watch something on television that you are interested in that's fine, go ahead and watch it. Then when the program has finished, turn the TV off and do something more useful with the time.

Can't Sleep

We looked at Moonlighting a couple of topics back. Time spent laying in bed at night unable to get to sleep, tossing and turning with your mind racing is another time-wasting activity.

So follow the advice and keep a pencil and paper by the bed. If you find yourself unable to sleep, turn the light on, make a note of your thoughts and you may find that helps you get back to sleep. If not use the time to think about some of your important tasks and note any thoughts down. That should do the trick!

Will It Work?

So that's six suggestions for using spare time that would otherwise be wasted. They may not all be right for you but any one of them will bring benefits and probably reduce stress, particularly for the waiting and travel time and times when you can't sleep.

Hot tip

Always keep your action list with you, then when you have spare time you will always be able to find something important to think about or work on.

Summary

- Our energy levels and alertness are not the same throughout the day, they rise and fall

- Quality time is the time (usually around four hours) when we are at the peak of our energy and alertness

- You can work out when your quality time is by keeping a record for a few days of how you are feeling every three hours

- We can sometimes come up with solutions or ideas that we hadn't even been working on during these periods

- Creative thinking is the process we follow to come up with new ideas or solve problems

- There are a number of stumbling blocks to creative thinking, such as: trying to find the one right answer, thinking logically, following rules or telling ourselves that we are not creative

- Learn to recognize these stumbling blocks and think positively to overcome them

- Allow your ideas to incubate if you get stuck by working on something else for a time and leaving it to your subconscious

- Insomnia can be a real problem but there are 15 proven tips to help, including winding down before going to bed and writing down concerns or bad thoughts

- One suggestion is to keep a note pad and pen by the side of the bed and write down anything that concerns or troubles you or keeps you awake. This will not only help you get to sleep but also means you will have some potentially useful notes in the morning

- The Pareto Principle or 80/20 Rule can be applied to most business activities by focusing on the most important 20% of activities

- It can also be applied to our quality time as this should be the 20% of our time that we use on important tasks

- Spare time, while waiting for a bus, train or plane, along with other wasted time, can always be put to good use

5 Getting Organized

If you are not organized, you will never be able to manage your time effectively. This chapter looks at organizing the workspace and everything you do in it to that end.

Your Workspace

Most knowledge workers and managers spend a large part of their working day at a desk in some sort of office. You might have the luxury of an individual office, share one with other co-workers, or increasingly it may be an office in your own home. Wherever you work, it makes sense to organize the work area in a way that increases your effectiveness.

Hot tip

Chapter 10 covers working from home in more detail, but these guidelines still apply to a home office.

Desk

Your desk should be positioned so that you have to turn away from it in order to face and speak to any visitor. This will make people more conscious of the fact that they are interrupting you. It will also prevent you from talking to them across your desk, which is a barrier to good communication.

Keep your work area tidy and preferably with pleasing pictures and some flowers or plants, it will improve your state of mind.

Windows

If you are right-handed try and have any source of natural light on your left and if you are left-handed on your right. Try not to have a window straight in front of you as it will be a distraction.

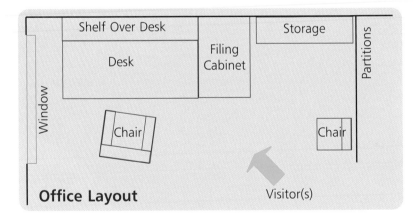

Office Layout

Lighting

Most offices have some form of overhead lighting but the use of a good quality desk lamp helps to reduce eye strain and headaches. It also has the effect of making people more conscious of your work area. Research has shown that people will actually walk more slowly and talk in a softer voice when they are in areas of localized lighting.

Chair

Make sure you have a comfortable chair and work at your sitting posture. But don't spend more than one hour sitting at your desk without getting up and moving about or stretching.

Desktop

Try to keep your desktop clear. Only have out the things you need for the task you are currently working on. Everything else should be filed away. Clear your desk completely every day before you leave the office.

Frequent Access Items

The things that you use a lot should be positioned as close to you as possible (preferably so that you can reach any of them without getting up from your desk). Anything that you use less often can be stored further away.

Filing System

Invest a little time in organizing your filing system in a way that supports the way you work. This should apply to hard copy filing and electronic filing systems. You should never have to search for things. There is a topic on filing systems on page 78.

Filing

Having organized your filing system you need to deal with new paper or electronic information effectively. The aim should be to handle each piece of paper once. Schedule this process once or twice a day and deal with everything, paper and electronic by sorting it into one of four categories:

Action

If something needs a quick answer or response do it right away while it's fresh in your mind. Otherwise add it to your action list to deal with later.

Information

Skim or read it as required then file it or throw it away.

Reading

Things that don't need to be dealt with straight away, save them for some marginal free time later.

Junk

If it's not one of the above three, then just bin it.

Effective Communication

We all spend a considerable amount of our time communicating in one way or another. On the telephone, email, in meetings and presentations and of course face to face. But for that communication to be effective, it must be more than just talking to people. That alone will not achieve effective communication.

It's Not What You Say

When we tell people something, we have not necessarily communicated what we intended to them. What we have communicated is what they have understood us to say. The two things are rarely the same.

People will put their own interpretation on things and that is what they will remember, if they remember anything at all! Research has shown that people generally only remember:

- 10% of what they read (text)
- 20% of what they hear
- 30% of what they see (illustrations or diagrams)
- 50% of what they see and hear

If we have to communicate something important, it's not enough just to send out a quick email. Better to go and see people, then tell them and show them what you want to communicate.

Get Some Feedback

People remember things better if they have spoken them as well as having heard them. If you ask them to verify that they have understood something, you also help them to remember it. But, if something is important, it should always be backed up in writing.

Common Understanding

If you have something important to communicate and want to achieve a common understanding, it makes sense to communicate with people in a group. For a department this will typically be a department meeting, or for a project team a project team meeting.

Then you can make sure there is a common understanding, by getting the group's confirmation of it. If there are differences they can be addressed and, hopefully, everyone will leave the meeting with the same message. All of these aids to effective communication build on each other.

68

Communication Methods

Oral communication, either one-to-one or in meetings, is only one of the many ways of keeping people in the picture. While it is excellent for important communications, it may not always be practical or we may also want to use other channels to back it up.

Email

This is probably the most frequently used (and abused) of the communication channels. There is a topic on email management on page 76.

Documents

The use of reports, instruction manuals and other forms of document are important if there is a lot of information to communicate. Effective writing on page 70 covers how to go about producing effective documents.

Other Channels

There are also bulletin boards, blogs, wikis, notice boards and other forms of information radiators. All of these are potentially valid ways of communicating.

Effective Communications

To communicate effectively, particularly when communicating orally, go through the following steps:

1 Understand clearly what you want to communicate and work out the most appropriate channel or channels

2 Prepare thoroughly and practice what you are going to say if you are communicating orally

3 Believe in what you are saying and be prepared to show it; if you don't you will be unconvincing and no one will believe what you say

4 Believe in success; you must believe that whatever you are saying will be successful, if not it will surely fail

Do this and you will be communicating effectively, whichever communications channel you use.

Don't forget

Reinforce your oral communication: tell people what you are going to say, say it and then tell them what you said.

Effective Writing

Writing is just one form of communication and to be effective your writing needs to achieve its purpose. So the first thing to establish is why you are proposing to write the document. Is it a sales proposal, is it a report to a team or to management, is it an instruction manual or just a letter to keep someone in the picture? Having established the purpose of the document, the second thing to be clear about is who it is for.

Audience

What is your intended audience? Is it one person, several people or even the whole organization? You may find it helpful if you try to visualize the readers in your mind's eye. Then you can phrase things in a suitable way for them.

Then try to pinpoint the message you want to convey to them. What is the key issue or question that needs to be answered? And what actions do you want the reader to take after reading it?

Writing

Once you have a clear understanding of the purpose and audience of the document, you can begin to list each of the thoughts you want to express. Then arrange the list by putting the points into a logical order and discarding any irrelevant ones. Develop the document by fleshing out each point and adding an introduction and summary. Lastly, fine tune the document, check it for spelling and punctuation and review it for good, plain English.

Plain English

To be effective, write conversationally (the way you would speak to someone) using short sentences and familiar words the reader will understand. Don't use any more words than are necessary and try to avoid any technical jargon and ambiguity.

Don't use acronyms unless you have to and then make sure you explain them the first time you use them. Use the active voice ("We did it") rather than passive voice ("It was done"). Use "your" rather than "our" and give suggestions rather than instructions to the reader.

KISS

This stands for 'Keep It Short and Simple'. Edit out any long repetitive or irrelevant sentences (aim for a maximum of 15 to 20 words). Try to keep letters to a single page.

Having established some overall guidelines, you can use the following steps as a checklist to produce an effective document:

1   Identify the purpose of the written communication, what the document is for

2   Define your intended audience, the person or people you are writing it for

3   Form a clear understanding of the message that you want to get across to them and what action you want them to take as a result of reading it

4   Make a complete list of all the points you want to make and the things you want to say

5   Arrange the list into a logical order, discarding any items that seem irrelevant to the purpose of the document

6   Flesh out each of the list of points using the plain English guidelines and fine tune them

7   Add an appropriate introduction explaining the purpose of the document and any highlights. This should be a single sentence in a one-page document or a paragraph in a larger document

8   Add an appropriate summary to the end of the document highlighting the conclusions and any recommended actions. Again this should be proportionate to the document from a single sentence to a paragraph

9   Review the finished document by reading it and checking the use of English, spelling and punctuation

10 Put your name, version number (if relevant) and the date of issue on the document, together with any other organization standard details and issue it

Hot tip

Unless it is a letter, review the document from time to time and update or withdraw it as necessary.

Effective Reading

Before you start reading anything, it makes sense to ask yourself why you're reading it. What do you want to get out of it? Then you can decide how much of your time you are prepared to give the exercise.

Cherry Picking

Start out by just reading the headings and introduction or summary and table of contents. These should tell you what the book or document covers and who it is intended for. Then you can decide if you need to read any more.

Skim Read

If you do decide you need to know more then skim read, don't read every word. The first and last paragraphs in each section will usually give a summary of sorts. The first and last sentences in each long paragraph likewise. Skim through, picking out any key words or concepts and looking at any diagrams and graphs (these often give a good summary).

Only read all the details if they are important to you.

Mark Up

When you do find something that is important, mark it up by highlighting or underlining key information and making notes in the margins. Doing this means you won't forget something important but clears your mind for the next chunk of text.

Then when you have finished the document or chapter go back and read it in more detail again later. This two-step approach will also help you to remember it.

If you are working with a document you have printed you can mark it up however you like, but if it's a book or a document that belongs to someone else use a soft pencil or sticky notes.

Effective Reading

To approach effective reading in easy steps:

1. Ask yourself why you are reading something and what you want to get out of it

2. Cherry pick the headings, introduction or summary and table of contents

3. If you need to know more, skim read the beginning and end of each section and the beginning and end of each paragraph

4. Look at any diagrams and graphs as these will often summarize what is in the text

5. Mark up anything of more interest and go back and read more of it once you have finished skimming

Types of Document

Different types of documents hold information in different ways and in different places in the document. They also have different breadths and depths of coverage. Understanding this difference will help you to get the most out of it in an effective way.

Newspapers and Magazines

These tend to give partial coverage of any given topic. Often they will feature the more interesting or exciting parts of a subject and ignore other information. However, the information excluded may be critical to a full understanding of the subject.

You may find that the most effective way of gathering information from newspapers and magazines is to cut out any relevant articles and file them. This way you will gather sets of articles that may, between them, explain the subject.

Technical Documents

If you have to read a large amount of technical material, you may find it useful to build up a glossary of terms as you work. You can then use it as you read through further material. Some people also find it helps their understanding to rewrite any difficult-to-grasp concepts in their own words.

When to Read

If reading and understanding something is critical, then it makes sense to do it when you are at your most alert, during your quality time. Otherwise reading for interest can be done whenever you have some free time available. If you do find something that turns out to be important, mark it up for reading later at a time when you are more alert again.

Don't forget

Use your quality time for only the most important and critical tasks.

Telephone Use

Do you know how much time you spend on the telephone? If you've carried out the time log and analysis exercise, you will do. If not keep a log of the time you spend on the phone for a couple of typical days. However much time you do spend on the phone you can make that time more effective.

Type of Phone

Most people these days have a desk phone and a mobile phone. The phone on your desk is the one you should use for preference as it is likely to have a number of useful functions:

- Voice mail or an answering machine: very useful for when you are out of the office or busy

- Caller ID: displays the number of the person calling or their name if you have their number stored on the phone

- Hands-free operation: a speaker so you can put the phone down and use your hands while talking or while on hold

- Plug-in headset: very useful if you spend a lot of time on the phone and/or work in a noisy office

- Speed dial: for numbers you call frequently

Voice Mail

Think about your voice mail message and what it says about you. You should record it yourself not use an anonymous message. Prepare a short script giving: your name, the fact that you cannot take the call at this time, asking the caller to leave their name and any message with their phone number if they would like you to call them back.

When you leave your office either put the phone onto voice mail or have it divert after a few rings. If you get a lot of interruptions by phone and need some quiet time to work on something, put your phone onto voice mail.

Making Calls

Plan your calls by listing the calls you need to make and then plan each call by writing down the key thing(s) you want to say so it is clear in your mind (similar to preparing to write).

Be ready if you are put through to their voice mail and leave a short message saying who you are, why you are calling, ask them

Hot tip

If your phone doesn't have these features, get one that does, it will save you time.

74

Don't forget

Remember to check your voice mail when you return to the office.

to call you back and give them your number. Do not try and explain anything in detail as it will sound long and rambling.

Batch your calls and set aside one or two blocks of time each day for making them. Some people find it helps to make calls just before lunch or the end of the day as people will be less inclined to talk at length and your calls will be quicker.

Get some form of timer (an egg timer or something electronic) and set yourself the goal of getting through each call in three minutes or less. You can do it without being rude.

Receiving Calls

If you are busy or have someone with you and don't want to be interrupted just divert the call to voice mail. If you are happy to take the call, pick the phone up quickly, smile and give your name, organization or department (if relevant) and ask how you can help the caller.

If you can deal with the call quickly (three minutes) and easily, then do so. If not then tell them that you will need to get some information together and agree a time when you will call them back. Do not put callers on hold for a long time while you go and find out something for them, it doesn't make good use of your time or theirs.

If you receive cold calls, sales calls, or other unwanted calls, interrupt them and be polite but tell them that you are not interested. If they persist just hang up. Scam calls, automated calls and fax machines, just hang up; there's no one there to upset.

Mobile Phones

Some phone systems now let you forward calls to your mobile phone rather than voice mail. Unless you are expecting an important call this is not a good idea. When taking calls on your mobile phone, particularly in a public space, be discreet or better still tell the caller that you are out of your office and will call them back on your return.

In meetings, with clients or in any other situation where you are working with or socializing with other people, turn off your mobile phone. It is the height of rudeness to answer your phone and get involved in another conversation while the people you are with sit patiently (or not) waiting for you to finish the call.

Beware

Thoughtless use of mobile phones can cause offence!

Email Management

Email is a really useful communications channel. It is quick, easy to use and informal. But it can also waste a lot of your time if you don't organize your use of it effectively.

Checking Your Email

How often do you check your email? Some people have their email program open all the time and, even worse, have it bleep when a new email arrives. They dive in eagerly to read the new bit of gossip only to be disappointed when they discover it's about work. But as they have started reading it they might as well finish it and reply. This is not effective use of their time.

Beware

Organize your email, don't let it organize you!

Decide how often you need to check your email. For most people this is no more frequently than twice a day. Set a regular time for this task, perhaps first thing in the morning and straight after lunch, and stick to it.

Inbox Management

When you open your email you are usually presented with your inbox, a list of messages with unread messages highlighted. It will also have the sender's name, the subject and an 'urgent' flag, so look down the list first to check for any potentially urgent messages. Then scan the remainder, decide what action you need to take on each and move it to the appropriate folder.

Folders

You may find it useful to set up email folders similar to your paper mail files, along the following lines:

- Action: emails that you need to do something about

- Information: emails that might contain something useful

- Reading: emails to read later

- Junk: your email should create one of these for you but just delete any junk email that gets into your inbox

Filters

Most email programs have facilities for filtering email to a junk mailbox. Use this feature but check your junk mail box from time to time in case anything got filtered that shouldn't have. Delete the junk and train the filter by telling it about junk that got into your inbox and anything in the junk folder that wasn't.

Address Book

Use your email program's address book feature for any regular contacts as this will save time in addressing email. Create address lists for any groups you send email to on a regular basis.

Email Format

You can personalize most email formats by selecting type fonts, size, color and even backgrounds. However, for business email, it is best to go for a neat, modern business look. A professional sans-serif font in black or dark blue with a plain white background is probably safest.

Standard Text

Signatures are the standard blocks of text that get inserted at the end of an email. Your full name, job title, organization and business phone number is usual. Some organizations add disclaimers, requests not to print email for environmental reasons, and advertising but it is best to keep this as short as possible.

For replies keep this signature text as brief as possible, or don't use one at all. After all they know who you are and who you work for already as they emailed you in the first place.

If you find you are often saying the same things in emails, then it is worth putting some standard paragraphs together in a text document or draft email that you can copy and paste from.

Email Etiquette

Never say anything in an email that you wouldn't be prepared to say openly in the office, in front of your boss.

- Keep emails short and if possible with just one subject

- When you are away set 'out of office' to auto reply or forward to a colleague. When you return check for any urgent emails

- Try not to use 'reply all' unless everyone on the distribution list really needs to know what you are saying

- Don't capitalize words (shouting) as it is considered rude

- Don't forward chain letters, virus warnings or spam

- Don't request read receipts, some people find it invasive and they can over-ride them anyway

Beware

Don't be tempted to go for handwriting or unusual fonts and fancy backgrounds, it just doesn't look professional.

Filing Systems

To be effective we need to be organized. To be organized we need somewhere to put things so that we can easily find them when we need them. That means some sort of filing system. The old adage used to be "a place for everything and everything in its place."

Stuff

We all have lots of stuff that accumulates over time. For instance, I now work out of a very small home office, so a lot of my stuff has ended up in the garage and attic. This is fine for old records and correspondence, but not if I suddenly find I need something in a hurry. So let's break stuff down a little:

Current Work

At any one time most of us are working on between three and ten important things. All the stuff associated with this current work should be right at hand when we need it. The system that seems to work for me is to have three levels of files:

Priority Tasks

The notes associated with the one task I am working on actively right now are in a clear (or color coded) transparent folder sitting on top of my desk. The notes for the other two to nine priority tasks are also in transparent plastic folders sitting in the top drawer of my desk. I can grab them immediately if I need to.

If I go off to a meeting that involves any of them I take the appropriate folder with me and put the others back in the top drawer. When I leave the office at night everything off the desk top goes straight into the top drawer.

Task Files

The supporting papers for each task are in a manila folder, labeled with the name of the task, in a suspense file in the bottom drawer of my desk. Papers tend to move between the plastic folder and suspense file as necessary while I am working on the task. All the papers are still right at hand when I need them, I just have to reach down a little further.

Completed Tasks

Once a priority task is completed the notes from the plastic folder go into the manila folder and the manila folder goes into my main filing cabinet. Filed by client, supplier, project or task name as appropriate.

Completed Work

Once you have completed a project or major piece of work, it makes sense to put all the stuff associated with it together. It needs to be somewhere you can find it fairly easily if you need to go back and review or revise anything. Again this could be filed by client, supplier or project as appropriate.

Correspondence

Letters, emails, notes of meetings with clients and suppliers and all manner of associated things need to be somewhere you can find them when you need to. These may start out as current work but once they have been dealt with move them into the appropriate client, supplier or project file.

Old Stuff

We all know that work expands to fill any available time. Well, over time, stuff has a terrible habit of expanding to fill any available space. Every so often you will need to weed out the old stuff you no longer need. I find doing this once a year during a quiet period (when a lot of people are on vacation) works well. But be prepared to be ruthless and treat nothing as sacred. Look at everything you are saving and ask yourself two questions:

1. Does this document, specification, letter, report or note need to be retained for a period of time for any legal reasons?

2. Does it need to be retained for any other sensible reason? Not nostalgia because you liked the project but maybe as a template for a similar future project

If the answer to either question was yes then put it into an archive box, clearly labelled with the contents and the date it needs to be retained until. Then send it to your archive store or put it in the garage/attic.

Otherwise put it in the shredding bin with no regrets. I personally find getting rid of unwanted baggage quite therapeutic.

Email

All of these points apply equally to email. Use the same filing structure on your email system and everything is synchronized.

Productivity Tools

We looked at organizers on page 50 and the use of office phones on page 74. We also touched briefly on some other productivity tools that might be applicable, these are:

Mobile Phone

Modern mobile phones (often referred to as smartphones) can do a lot more than make and receive telephone calls over a radio link whilst moving around. They also support text messaging, email, internet access, short-range communications, business applications, photography and even gaming. Used wisely, they can be a great aid to effectiveness.

Notebooks

Some people still use paper notebooks but increasingly notebook computers (small laptops) and netbook computer (scaled down laptops) designed for mobile use are the notebooks of choice. They integrate the typical components of a desktop computer into a single, compact unit. They are powered by mains electricity but can be used away from an outlet using a rechargeable battery. Netbooks have no moving disk and are therefore smaller, lighter and have better battery life than notebooks. They are a tremendous aid to working on the road.

Personal Organizer

Originally a small ring binder containing a diary, calendar, address book and other sections for notes. These physical personal organizers have largely been replaced by electronic personal organizers or personal digital assistants (PDAs). These have applications similar to PC organizers and the ability to access the Internet using wireless connectivity, with a web browser and email software. They also have audio capabilities enabling their use as a portable media player. Most can also be used as mobile phones and the distinction between PDAs and smart phones is blurring rapidly.

They are even more compact that a netbook computer but not so convenient for word processing or spreadsheets due to the absence of a proper keyboard.

Printer

An office printer (normally laser) is a computer peripheral that rapidly produces high quality text and graphics on plain paper. The more advanced models include high resolution, high quality color printing for images and text and even collation and stapling of documents. An excellent aid to office efficiency.

Scanner

An image scanner is a device that optically scans images, text, handwriting or even solid objects and converts them to a digital image. The most common are the flatbed scanners where the item to be copied is placed, face down on a glass window for scanning. There are also portable hand-held scanners (good for small quantities of text or image) and mechanically-driven scanners (good for feeding large documents that wouldn't fit on a flatbed scanner).

Scanners can effectively act as a photocopier (with the output copy being sent to a printer), an image capture device (similar to microfilm) or, coupled with optical character recognition (OCR) software, they can convert a text image into text that can be processed by word processing software.

Multi-Function Printers

Multi-function or all-in-one devices are office machines which incorporate the functionality of multiple devices into one box. They range from small footprint devices for a home or small business environment to large centralized document management systems for a large-office environment. They provide printing, scanning, photocopying, facsimile (fax) and email functions.

USB Memory Stick

The USB memory stick (or flash drive) is a small data storage device that integrates flash memory with a USB plug, from which they also draw their power. It has replaced the floppy disk as the most convenient way of transporting data and software. It provides the same function but without the need for a disk drive, just a USB socket. It has much greater capacity and is more reliable as there are no moving parts.

Scheduling Tools

Microsoft Project and similar scheduling tools provide project planning, scheduling and control functionality. They can also manage resource allocation and provide what-if scenarios to enable various planning options to be explored. No project manager would attempt to run a serious project without the aid of a good scheduling tool.

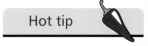

Hot tip

Always carry a USB memory stick with you, it makes it so easy for someone to give you a copy of an important document or file.

Summary

- Most of us spend a large part of our working days at a desk in an office, so it makes sense to organize your work area to increase your effectiveness

- Use light effectively and keep your work area clean and tidy

- Effective communication starts with understanding what you want to communicate and then selecting the most appropriate method or methods

- Effective writing involves determining the purpose and the intended audience, then developing the communication using plain English and keeping it as short as possible

- You can read more effectively by using techniques such as cherry picking, skimming and marking up text

- Modern telephone systems provide a number of functions that can improve your effectiveness

- Plan phone calls in advance and make them in planned blocks of time to make them more effective

- Deal with receiving calls in a planned way and be prepared to divert calls to voice mail when you are busy

- When using a mobile phone be aware of others and turn your phone off when you are in meetings

- Schedule time for regularly checking email a couple of times a day and use folders to stream emails for action, information or reading later

- Use email filters, address book and standard blocks of text to make your email time as effective as possible and follow the email etiquette

- To be effective you need to stay on top of your filing systems and have everything you need for priority tasks near at hand

- Be ruthless about deciding what old stuff to keep and, unless there is a strong reason for retaining something, shred it

- Other productivity tools can aid your efficiency and effectiveness in the office and on the road

6 Saying No

This chapter deals with the difficult subject of saying no, but in the right way.

Why is it Difficult?

This is one of the shortest chapters in the book, but also one of the most important. Learning how to say no in the right way is critical to making effective use of your time, but it is also difficult.

Do you have difficulty in saying no to people? Well don't worry, you are not alone, most of us have the same problem.

Why is it so Hard?

What is so difficult about saying no to people? Well to start with the person who is asking you may be disappointed, upset or even angry at you for refusing their request. Presumably you want to continue working with that person and you may even need to ask them for something in future. That could all be put at risk if you upset them by saying no in the wrong way.

Before you can learn how to say no in the right way you need to understand why you find it difficult. These are some of the common reasons people give:

Wanting to Help

Most of us want to help other people. We are kind and friendly and it seems the right thing to do. It feels uncomfortable to turn someone down so we try to help them even though we can't really spare the time.

Wanting to be Liked

We don't want to feel alienated from our colleagues by being disagreeable. We want them to like us so we accede to their requests even though we know we shouldn't because of our other work commitments.

Afraid of Being Rude

Many of us were taught as children that it is rude to say no, especially to adults. So as adults we continue to think this way, especially to people who are 'senior' to us in the organization or customers. We don't want to appear rude so we end up saying yes even though we don't want to.

Afraid of Conflict

We are afraid we might make the person asking us angry if we turn them down. This could end up in a confrontation now or at some future time. So we overcome our reluctance and give in. We agree to help them against our better judgement.

Closing Doors

We are worried that saying no means closing doors. If we refuse to do something now, it might mean that we will be considered unhelpful. At some future time people will remember this and perhaps not consider us for a promotion or some other new opportunity that might come along.

Burning Bridges

If we say no it might alienate the person asking us as they see it as a sign of rejection. But we don't want to burn all our bridges and ruin our relationship, so once again we give in.

Whatever the reason for our deciding to give in to the request, and often against our better judgement, we go ahead and do what we've been asked. Then as they say, we live to regret it as we get further behind with our other work.

Sooner or later we miss a critical deadline or the quality of our work deteriorates and we are blamed for that. No one will be interested in the fact that you caused the problem by trying to help someone.

How We Wish

Once we have identified that we should be saying no, we often start to identify opportunities in the past where we should have said no but didn't. Most of us have, at some time or another, told ourselves that we should never have agreed to do something and wondered why we did it. We somehow get the feeling that we have let a golden opportunity slip.

But the good news is that if you go through this experience often enough you will start to learn from it. You will begin to understand that you should be making a stand and start to say no more often. We will be looking at ways of reinforcing this in the next topic.

Conflicting Emotions

One final thing that can make it hard to say no, is having already said no once and then felt bad about it afterwards. We might have upset the person or made them angry.

We might now be seen as a 'difficult person'. We just feel that we can't go through that process all over again.

Hot tip

Be honest with yourself and admit that you should have said no and will start to make a stand next time.

Why We Should

If you found yourself in agreement with some of the reasons for not saying no in the previous topic, you are not alone. They have probably applied to all of us at some time or another. But these reasons are often misconceptions as saying no doesn't mean you are being rude or disagreeable. It doesn't mean that you have committed some irrevocable act and burnt all of your bridges. You can say no and you will say no and these are some of the reasons:

Work Overload

Do you have too much work to do? If you answered the checklist on page 26 you will know the answer to this. If you do, then once again you are not alone. Many of us are overworked and therefore over stressed as well.

By saying yes to additional commitments for any of the reasons in the previous topic you will be making things even worse. The easy way to help this situation out is to learn to say no to taking on any additional commitments.

Working Late

By saying yes to additional commitments you now have even more work to do. If something else isn't going to slip you will find yourself working later and later to catch up again.

Look around you. Is the person who you said yes to still there, is anyone else still there? If not then you are paying a high price for saying yes. Next time just say no.

Letting People Down

If you don't work extra hours to make up for the additional commitments something else is going to suffer. You are going to be letting someone else down. That could be your boss, a customer, another department or another colleague.

By saying yes to one person you have let another person down. It really doesn't make sense if you think about it. You know you should have said no, so next time do it.

Letting Yourself Down

By saying yes when you should be saying no you will end up spending a lot of your valuable time and energy doing things for other people. You might not even get any credit for it. That means you are not spending as much time as you should be for yourself.

Doing that will mean you end up feeling very frustrated and the only person you can blame is yourself. If you want to do your job well and have some personal time, you simply must learn how to say no.

Poor Productivity

If you end up taking on too many commitments, you will either not get things done in time (missed work deadlines) or you will have to cut corners (poor quality work). Either of these will result in your work being assessed as poor and that is going to increase your level of stress.

But new requests are typically coming in all the time. If you are going to stay productive and reduce your stress level, there is no other option than learning how to say no. Now is the time to make that commitment, you are going to learn how to say no.

Avoiding Work Overload

The first step is to check that you really do have too much to do rather than what you are doing is ineffective. The second step is to make sure you are dealing with the important priority work before dealing with any of the additional work. Then go and see your boss, explain the situation and arrange to get rid of the overload.

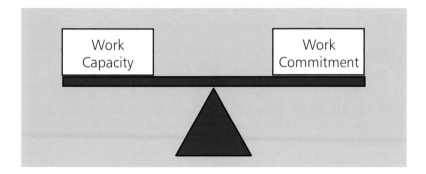

Get your working life back in balance. There are only so many hours in the day. Whatever you choose to do with your time limits your ability to do other things.

Every time someone asks you to do something additional, ask yourself if it is more important than the thing you will have to give up in order to do it. And that thing might be your free time, health and happiness.

Just Say No

It sounds easy enough to say it, but it is one of the key things you can learn that will make you more effective. Learning how to say no takes time but it gets easier as you go along. People will also begin to realize that you are not a 'soft touch'.

It's OK to say No

Don't feel bad about saying no, it's your right, no matter who is asking you and what the situation is. Rather than think you can't say no, learn how to say it in a way that the other person can understand and accept. Tell them why you are saying no. Explain about your work commitments and the impact saying yes would have on your priority work.

Be firm and polite but not defensive or overly apologetic. This shows that you are sympathetic, but will not easily change your mind if pressured.

Don't Change Your Mind

They may try to persuade you to change your mind, but don't! Listen politely to whatever they say, reflect it back to them and tell them that you understand their problem, but the answer is still no. Tell them you're sorry you can't help and hope they can find another way around the problem.

Avoid Bad Body Language

Don't let your words tail off or put your hand over your mouth while you speak. Don't look away from them while you are talking, it makes you look insincere. Keep an open relaxed posture, relaxed eye contact and an upright posture.

Feel Good About It

Feel good, you are making the best use of your time for your priority work and your organization.

Is it the Boss?

If it is your boss or someone senior, you can still say no. It's still your choice even though it is not an easy one. We will be looking at how to go about this in the next topic.

As you begin to say no, you will soon realize that it's not as bad as you thought it was going to be. Other people will be understanding and will often accept it at face value. The fear of saying no is just in our minds.

Here are a few other suggestions for ways of saying no that might help you the first few tricky times:

Not a Good Time

You will quite often get sudden requests for help when you are in the middle of something. Tell them it's not a good time for you as you are working on something else. This is only a temporary hold up and you are letting them know that you may be able to help them some other time.

I Would Like to Help, But

This lets them know that you like their suggestion (but only say this if you mean it). Then follow up with one of the other reasons.

Let Me Think About It

This is a maybe rather than a no. Again it buys you some time to think about the ramifications before you make the final decision. But let them know when you will get back to them and make sure you do so.

I'll Keep It In Mind

If it's something you don't want to do, let them know it's not right for you, but tell them you'll keep it in mind. They will know there is nothing wrong with what they are asking and that you might be open to future requests.

I'm Not the Best Person to Ask

If you can't contribute much or don't have the resources, let them know. And if you are aware of someone else who might be able to, suggest them. That way they will see that you are trying to help.

No I Can't

The simplest and most direct way is just to say no. Don't stop to think about it, just say no. You will often find their reaction is much better than you had previously feared.

Learn to say no and, once you do, you'll find how easy it really can be. You'll have more time for work and your private life. You'll be less stressed and you will enjoy life more.

It's all about how you say no, rather than the fact you're saying no, that affects the outcome. Saying no is respecting and valuing your time. It is your right. It will reduce your stress levels and give you time for what's really important.

What About The Boss?

In this chapter we have seen why we find it hard to say no, why we should say no and how to do it the right way. That's all well and good I hear you say but what about the boss? About.com Career Planning offers the following advice:

Saying No to Your Boss

Your boss just assigned a new project, with a tight deadline, to you and you are already overloaded with other work. If you try to do it something is going to slip. But can you say no to your boss?

Questions to Ask Yourself

Ask yourself the following questions before you decide to say no to your boss:

1. Do I already have several other important tasks that will not leave me enough time for this new one?

2. Do I have the ability to delegate enough of my other work to leave me time for this new assignment?

3. Am I able to put some of my other work on hold while I concentrate on this new one?

4. If I take on this new assignment will it have a negative impact on my other work?

5. Do I have the required abilities or skills to carry out this new assignment?

6. Is there anyone else who is capable of carrying out this new assignment?

There are good reasons and bad reasons to say no and you should consider these before making a final decision.

Good Reasons to Say No

If your boss is a reasonable person, he or she should be able to understand the following reasons:

- I won't have enough time to work on it, even if I come in to work early and work late

- My other work will suffer if I have to take on this additional work assignment

- I don't have the right skills or experience to do this work and I won't be able to complete it in time

Bad Reasons To Say No

The following reasons are probably not good enough:

- I think it looks too difficult

- It's not part of my job description

- I'm right in the middle of planning my wedding and can't focus on anything else right now

If you do make your mind up to say no, you then need to think about how you are going to tell your boss.

How to Say No

Prepare thoroughly before you go and see your boss. Make sure you do have a good reason or reasons for saying no and make a list of all the other priority work you have to do. Treat the session with your boss as a negotiation rather than an outright rejection. And don't leave things to the last minute, so that your boss has enough time to assign the work to someone else if that is what they decide to do.

Start by explaining your reasons thoroughly so that your boss can see that you have considered the situation carefully. List the other priority work commitments you have and explain why you can't delegate any of it.

If you believe that your other work will suffer if you take on this assignment, explain that to your boss. They should appreciate your honesty and your commitment to your other projects.

If it is because you don't have the right skills, admit it to your boss. Again your boss should appreciate your honesty and may even arrange some training for you.

Your boss now has three choices: they can re-assign some of your other work, help you delegate some of your other work, or reassign the new project to someone else.

Don't forget

Be completely honest with your boss, it will pay off in the long run.

Summary

- Most people have problems with saying no, as by nature we want to help others and not let them down

- There are many reasons why, against our better judgement, we end up saying yes when we should be saying no

- Many of us are already overworked so by saying yes when we should be saying no we are making things even worse for ourselves

- We end up working later and later, letting other people down and letting ourselves down by missing deadlines or allowing the quality of our work to deteriorate

- If you do have too much work, the first step in the process of rectifying the situation is to talk to your boss and arrange to get rid of the overload

- Then you need to face up to the consequences of saying yes which results in your having to work late, letting yourself down and poor productivity

- Make sure that you are focusing on the important priority work items before dealing with any additional work

- Learn how to say no politely but firmly and explain your reasons for doing so

- There are a number of ways you can soften the refusal by explaining that it is not a good time, you don't have the right skills or that you would have liked to help but can't

- The most direct way is just to say no and once you have learned to do this it will get easier and easier

- Saying no to your boss can be quite a bit harder but it can be done if you have a good reason for it such as: not having enough time, the negative impact it will have on your other work or not having the right skills or experience

- Prepare carefully before approaching your boss and be prepared to negotiate on your other work

- If you don't have the right skills be prepared to admit it, your boss may be able to help

7 Distractions

Interruptions are one of the biggest distractions we face. But while we can't prevent them, we can minimize their impact.

The Cost of Interruptions

Make no mistake about it, interruptions are costly. It has been calculated that the average knowledge worker spends around a quarter of their working time in dealing with interruptions. So take a quarter of your salary and double it (to allow for business overheads) and that's how much your interruptions cost.

They have even coined a new term 'attention management' for the process of dealing with interruptions.

Interruptions
In terms of the types of interruptions we have to deal with, there are four main sources:

- Drop-in Visitors: these tend to have the most significant impact on us as we have to turn to face them, which completely interrupts what we were doing

- Phone Calls: nearly as bad as drop-in visitors as we have to use at least one hand to hold the phone and this has an impact on what we can do

- Email: almost as disruptive as phone calls and a lot of people handle emails in a very ineffective manner

- Distractions: anything that distracts us from what we are doing, either external (noise or image) or internal (our own thoughts or concerns)

Every time you have to deal with an interruption you will have to break off from whatever you were doing and then get back into it again after the interruption. This can waste as much time as the actual interruption itself.

The Interrupter
You can try locking yourself away somewhere, without a phone and with a 'do not disturb' sign on the door and I can almost guarantee someone will still manage to interrupt you. But consider this: you do the same thing when you interrupt someone else. Now I assume that you would only do it if the matter was important. But important to whom, you or the interruptee?

Urgent or Important?
We have already looked at the question of important versus urgent. Your question may be important, but if it's not urgent it

Don't forget

Important and urgent tasks take top priority, followed by important but not urgent tasks.

could wait. Someone else might have a really urgent question, but it might not be important. If you are going to be effective with your time you need to understand the difference so that you can prioritize your response.

Cumulative Impact

If we just had one single interruption it would not be so bad, but interruptions sometimes seem to be continuous. It is no wonder that we have difficulty getting critical tasks completed if we are constantly being interrupted and then having to try and get back to where we were.

The Working Environment

There have been significant changes in the way we work over the past 10 years and these changes are likely to continue. In addition to phones (most of us have at least two) and voicemail we have email and instant text messaging. From working in our own office we can now be working anywhere from a home office, our car, a hotel room, an airport lounge or a customer site.

Our co-workers can be located anywhere across different time zones and national borders. The next interruption could come from anywhere. I had one client in California who would regularly call me on a Friday afternoon at 5:30 just as I was packing up for the week, with a cheery "Good morning John", it being half past nine in the morning there!

The Impact of Interruptions

A study into interrupted work by the University of California and Humboldt University showed that people who are constantly interrupted end up working harder and faster to compensate for the time they lost by being interrupted.

After 20 minutes of interrupted performance the subjects reported significantly higher stress, frustration, workload, effort and time pressure. This in turn has its cost as the interrupted work may have been completed by working harder, but at the price of additional stress and frustration. There is also the high possibility of a reduced quality of work.

We can still be our own worst enemy. When asked how quickly they respond to a new email notification, only 35% said when convenient, the remainder said immediately or shortly thereafter.

Hot tip

Close your email until the time you scheduled for checking it.

Minimizing the Impact

If we use the same logic to handle interruptions as we did for creating our action list (page 48), we need to consider if an interruption is urgent and important. If so we should deal with it, if not it should be deferred. And if something is important, who is it important to? Is it important to the interrupter, to your group or to the whole organization?

Your Mind Set

You need to start by changing your mind set and get out of the react mode of dealing with things immediately they happen. Unless it is both urgent and important it is more effective to schedule it into your day plan for some later time.

You need to stay focused on the task you are working on until you complete it. The issues and problems will still be there when you have finished.

Guidelines

Set up some personal guidelines for how you will deal with any interruptions:

- Who you are prepared to interrupt your work for and who will have to wait

- Stand up to greet people who interrupt you so that you control the conversation

- Ask them how long their interruption will take so that you can decide whether to handle it now or later

- Ask yourself if you need to be the person to handle it, if not, delegate it to someone else

- Ask them if you need to deal with the problem right now, if not, schedule a time to deal with it later

- When you do get interrupted, leave yourself a note of where you were to make it easier to get back there

Self-Defense

Surveys have found that simple tactics like closing the door and diverting phones to voicemail can be very effective in combating interruptions. When you schedule time for important tasks in your day plan, let people know you are unavailable. If you have your own office, close the door and put up a 'do not disturb' sign.

If you don't have your own office, make sure your desk faces away from the direction that people will approach you in (so they don't catch your eye). Divert your phone to voicemail and close your email. If someone asks if they can have a quick chat, say no.

In return for this 'do not disturb' time, set 'open door' hours for when people can drop-in and ask you questions. Then reschedule any unexpected visitors for this time.

Don't forget

See Your Workspace (on page 66) for how to set up your office or work area.

Minimizing Interruptions

While you can't prevent interruptions you can plan to minimize unwelcome interruptions:.

1 Offer them five minutes now (and stick to it) or a scheduled meeting later

2 Tell them that you are busy working on something important. After all, you *are*

3 Stand up and if they sit down take a perch on the edge of your desk

4 Meet in their office if you can, then you can decide when to leave

5 Avoid all small talk when you're busy as it doubles the interruption time

6 Get them to come to the point, be polite but firm. "Be ruthless with time but gracious with people"

7 Listen well and try to help them (don't send them away empty-handed)

8 Have a clock available where they can see it and don't be afraid to look at it from time to time

9 If it is a telephone call ask them to call you back at a more convenient time (your scheduled phone time)

Managing Interruptions

Drop-in visitors and phone calls are the biggest wasters of time, because they happen all the time and are hard to resist. "Do you have a minute?" conversations never take one minute and the average phone call takes around six minutes. Yet, when asked, most people believe they could complete the call in two minutes if they were more effective. But the phone is easy, just divert it to voicemail while you're busy, drop-in visitors are not so easy.

Prevention

They say that prevention is better than cure, so can you prevent drop-in visitor interruptions altogether? Establish clear boundaries around the time you have scheduled for your priority work. Close the door, divert your phone to voicemail and let your team know that you're not available and when you will be available again. Also schedule regular meetings with your key team members so that they don't need to interrupt you so often.

The Interruption

But whatever you do you will get interruptions. So accept that interruptions are a fact of life. They are just going to happen. So when they do, don't let yourself feel thrown off track. Try these steps for effectively handling drop-in visitors:

1. Start by making a quick note of where you are on your current task so you can get back to it after dealing with the interruption

2. Stop looking at your computer, put down anything you are holding, take a deep breath and give the interrupter your full attention. Although this sounds counter-intuitive, they've got you so you may as well listen, it might just be important

3. Turn to face them, make eye contact and listen carefully to what they are saying

4. Stand up to talk to them, conversations will be shorter if you're standing rather than sitting

5. If they want to discuss something that isn't urgent, then schedule a time to talk to them later

6   If they are rambling on, ask them how you can help them, this will help them get to the point

7   Ask yourself if you are the best person to deal with it, if not tell them who is

8   If you can give them a quick answer, do it, if not make a note of the issue and tell them you will get back to them and make sure you do

9   Ask them to email you all the details if it is a lengthy problem, with their recommendations for action

Don't forget

You have the right to say no!

Other Actions

Keep a record of all the interruptions you get for a week or two. Record the date, time, by whom you were interrupted, the issue and whether it was important and/or urgent. This will let you identify when interruptions happen most often and who the most frequent interrupters are.

Having captured the details, you can then assess how the interruptions impacted on you and how you could better manage them or minimize their impact. Other steps you can take include:

1   Keep your action list with you and make sure you go straight back to where you left off after the interruption

2   Assume you will get interrupted, so make sure you allow time for it in your daily schedule

3   Think before you interrupt anyone else. By minimizing your interruptions, you will improve the overall productivity of the organization

Control

You can take control to effectively manage interruptions. When you allow for them in your schedule, know where they are coming from and apply strategies to minimize their impact, you will be on the way to effective time management and a productive work life.

The Worst Offender

Interruptions are not the only form of interference in the workplace. Distractions may cause less interference, but they do prevent you from getting on with your planned work at the usual pace. The person who distracts you most often is actually yourself. You stop to make coffee, drop in to see someone for a quick chat or drop the task you are currently working on and start another. Does it sound familiar?

Interruptions and distractions of any sort (such as daydreaming, thinking about other things you have to do or even just taking a break) cause you to abandon what you are currently working on, leaving it unfinished. This can create problems or stress for co-workers relying on the completion of your work.

Why We Get Distracted

It is very easy to get distracted, it's the way we are. One minute we are working away at some critical task, then a thought about something totally different drifts into our head and we are away with the fairies. There was probably nothing wrong with the task we were working on, it's just the distraction was a bit more interesting.

Dealing With Distractions

Learning how to deal with distractions is critical to effective time management. If distractions cost you one hour per working day, that is 240 hours per year or six 40-hour weeks.

We need something to bring us back to the moment. Carol Gignoux of ADD Insights recommends using a pad and paper. She calls it her 'capture pad' but a yellow sticky note pad would be equally good.

When a distraction happens just write the distraction down on your note pad and carry on with the task at hand. It doesn't need to be 'War and Peace' just the topic 'sales figures' or 'check bank balance'. When you complete the task have a look at your note pad and follow up on any distractions that need attention.

Critical Distractions

From time to time the distraction might be more important than the task you are working on. In which case, make a note on your pad about where you were with the task and what you have to do next. Then you can give the distraction your full attention and

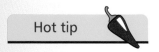

Hot tip

Keep a note pad by you all the time at work for recording distractions and interruptions.

know when you eventually get back to the original task, you will know exactly where you were.

This can also be a good technique for other interruptions like drop-in visitors and phone calls.

Ground Rules

Set yourself some ground rules for how you will deal with distractions. Making sure that you can stay focused on your work is crucial but it will require good self-discipline:

1. The capture pad is a good starting point so implement that right now

2. Keep your action list in sight all day and cross off each task as you complete it

3. Break big tasks down into a number of sub-tasks of around 10 minutes duration. These will act as stepping-stones to keep you on track, even if you get distracted.

4. If a critical distraction crops up, finish your current sub-task first so that when you return to it later you can move on to the next sub-task

5. Don't leave your email program running all the time, restrict yourself to checking your email two or three times a day, to avoid getting sidetracked

6. If you do have to access the Internet for anything concerning your work, be careful not to get distracted from your purpose

Face up to the fact that opportunities for self-distraction are everywhere. Checking the news, weather, Facebook, blogs, Wikipedia and so on. It's not their fault, it's yours. So face up to it and take it in hand.

Never be tempted to play any computer games during your work time. Disable or remove any that are installed on your computer if you can.

Beware

The Internet provides a huge source of ready-made distractions!

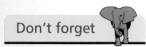

Procrastination is the thief of time.

Fear of Failure

One of the biggest reasons for procrastination can be the fear of failure. Some people have an irrational fear that they will not succeed. This could be based on uncertainty about the future, not wanting to let important people down or just a lack of self-confidence. Maybe they tried it once before and it went wrong. Maybe it's something they have never done before and are afraid they might not get it right first time. One thing is certainly true, the higher the fear of failure the more we tend to procrastinate.

Some people on the other hand, who have a strong feeling of self-belief, competence and a strong degree of autonomy, are much less likely to procrastination. If we feel competent and have the ability to learn new skills, we will feel more capable. So how do you go about fostering that feeling of competence?

No Fear

You have nothing to fear except fear itself, so you need to focus on your past successes, not your failures. You need to remember the times when things worked, not when they failed.

Be Willing to Fail

The fear of failure can stop us achieving our full potential. In a world of uncertainty, it's not difficult to see why so many people tend to play it safe. But this brings its own risks, as if you don't stretch yourself and risk failing, your success will be limited.

Most of us underestimate our ability to recover from failure and therefore pass up on valuable opportunities. This ability to fail has been seen as a mark of the truly successful. It's not unacceptable to fail, we learn through failure. We try new things and if they fail we learn from it and change our approach.

Erin Falconer (editor in chief of Pick the Brain) recommends the following strategies to overcome the fear of failure:

1 Missed opportunity cost: the potential benefits you lose by avoiding high risk opportunities. With no risks, you can live a quiet life, but you are unlikely to make your mark on the world

2 Check out the alternatives: the unknown is a major source of fear and the potential consequences can seem far worse than they actually are. Take a look at all the

potential outcomes (both good and bad) so that you can understand both the benefits of success and the risks of failure

3 Look at the worst case: if you go for it and fall flat on your face, how long will it take you to get over it? The answer may be a lot better than you think. If the worst comes to the worst, you could probably find another job in a couple of months, or would you rather stay in mediocrity forever?

4 The benefits of failure: life is a series of experiments, the more you make, the more you learn. Every failure is an opportunity for growth. Many managers at large companies would prefer to hire someone who has tried to start their own business and failed rather than someone who spent their time in a safe job

5 Contingency plan: overcome the fear of failure by developing a plan B that you will switch to if plan A fails. If you manage risk intelligently, you can get the benefits of high-risk opportunities but with a safety net

6 Take action: this is the best way to reduce fear and build confidence, for as soon as you do, you'll begin accumulating experience and knowledge. The first time is always the hardest but, once you've done it, you start to build your self-confidence

7 Burn your boats: the ancient Greeks traveled across the sea to do battle and the first thing they did after landing was to burn the boats. With no way to get home besides victory, they had no choice but to follow through, so go for it and don't look back

Trial and error is they way that we learn to solve problems. To make an error is not to fail, but to take one more step on the path to final success. Treat things as learning experiences and be prepared to fail. Then reflect on the outcome and plan for how you will do it better next time.

Hot tip

Don't be afraid of failing, just go for it and, if it does fail, learn from it.

Making Decisions

After the fear of failure, having to make decisions is the next biggest cause of procrastination. Some things in life are very clear cut and easy to make decisions about. You can see a train speeding towards you, you want to live, so you don't try to cross the tracks. But other decisions are not so straightforward. Should you apply for a new job? Should you move house? Should you get married and, if so, to whom?

Life is Ambiguous

Things are very rarely clear cut and sometimes any decision can be right or wrong. The problem is, that if we wait until we are absolutely certain before taking an action, we may never act. Sometimes there is no one right decision, just a number of alternatives. Trying to find the one right decision assumes that life is always simple. Some people just freeze like a rabbit caught in the headlights of a car.

One of the problems with not making a decision is that it increases stress and tension through worry. Some of the most common pitfalls are:

Paralysis by Analysis

Some people just can't make a decision to save their life. They write down all the positive and negative reasons for doing something and they still can't decide. They ask other people for advice and yet still can't make up their mind. They know they need to make a decision but don't know how to go about it. And if they do finally make a decision they agonize about whether it is the right one or not.

No Decision is a Decision

Other people constantly obsess about what they should do 'for the best'. Should they try and make the best of a bad situation and hang in there or should they leave and find another job? They want someone else to make the decision for them. The trouble is they may be trying to make a binary decision out of a multiple choice question. And of course all the time they fail to make a decision they are effectively deciding to stay.

Wanting Certainty

Some people have a simplistic idea of what is right and wrong. They don't feel they can act on a decision while they still have any doubts about it. They want absolute certainty and official approval.

When this doesn't happen, they go over and over it again in their minds and start to fret about it far too much.

Emotional Decisions

Making decisions based on some sort of whim. These decisions can often be recognized as mistakes, but the person responsible will rarely admit it and will try to back up their decision with emotional rationalization. They 'know' they can change a violent abuser through their love. They 'know' they will disappoint too many people if they do not agree to a proposed change.

Need for Approval

Some believe their decision can only be correct if it is approved by other people. They are afraid of making an independent decision. In short they are afraid of growing up and taking adult responsibility for their actions.

Failing to Learn

Making the same mistakes over and over due to a failure to learn from the past. These people will rarely admit that they have failed to learn, blaming fate, a lack of support from colleagues, the time wasn't right for it or any other reason other than themselves.

How to Make a Decision

Making a decision is not that difficult once you have decided you are going to make one:

1. Trust your instincts and don't always try to find logical reasons for everything, if it feels right, go for it!

2. Keep your emotions out of it, intuitive decision making works best when you don't get emotionally involved

3. Use your imagination, envisage living with the decision and decide how it makes you feel

4. Once you've made the decision get on and implement it right away

5. Accept that you will make some wrong decisions, but you can still learn from them

Summary

- The average knowledge worker spends around a quarter of their working time dealing with interruptions

- The major sources of interruption are drop-in visitors, phone calls, email and other distractions (external or internal)

- Dealing with an interruption takes the time of the interruption plus the same amount of time to get back to where you were before the interruption

- People respond to being interrupted by working harder and faster to compensate, but this increases stress, frustration and time pressure

- You need to change your mind set from react mode to focusing on your critical tasks until they are completed

- While you can combat interruptions you can't eliminate them altogether so plan to minimize their impact

- No matter how hard you try you will still get drop-in visitors when you are trying to focus on a critical task so be prepared

- Record the interruptions you get for a couple of weeks so that you can plan to manage them or minimize their impact

- When it comes to distractions we are the worst offender ourselves and no matter how hard we try to stay focused other thoughts will drift into our heads

- Keep a note pad by you and just jot down any stray distractions to look at later and immediately get back to the task in hand

- If the distraction is more critical than the task in hand, reverse the procedure and note where you were on the task

- Set yourself some ground rules for dealing with distractions and beware of the Internet!

- Fear of failure can hold you back from achieving your full potential, so be prepared to fail and learn from it

- Failing to make decisions can similarly hold you back, so trust your judgment and make decisions

8 Effective Meetings

This chapter looks at why so many meetings are bad meetings and how we can make sure our meetings are effective and make best use of everyone's time.

Not Another Meeting!

How often do we hear the cry "Meetings, bloody meetings!" as people rush from one meeting straight to another. We need to have meetings in order to function effectively as a group or team. They are one of the most effective means of communication, but they need to be controlled if they are not going to waste everyone's precious time.

Poorly-run meetings are one of the top time wasters cited in surveys. People feel that their time is being wasted, which they resent. That leads to general dissatisfaction, frustration and ultimately staff turnover.

On Time?

Let me ask you a question: do the meetings you organize and those you attend always begin on time? We looked at some of the problems with ineffective meetings back on page 25. Among a number of other problems we listed people arriving late, particularly if it happens to include the person running the meeting. So if your meetings don't start on time ask yourself why not? And is there something you should do about it?

Do You Really Need It?

Quite often one meeting can spawn another. A topic gets raised that's not in the scope of the current meeting, or the right people to deal with it are not at the meeting. So another meeting gets called. Before calling a meeting try asking yourself if you really need it:

1. Consider the real cost of the meeting: and not just the cost in terms of salaries and overheads, it's more a question of is it the best way for the organization to use people's time?

2. Is there a better way or a more effective way of doing it, such as by telephone conference call or an email?

3. Only invite the people you need: if you come to the conclusion that it must be a meeting, then make sure you only invite the people who really need to be there

If you can tick all three of these boxes then go ahead and schedule the meeting.

Meeting Invites

Ask yourself if you need to attend all the meetings you end up going to. Carry out a review of all the meetings you attend and use a checklist to identify if you really need to be there or if you only need to attend part of the meeting. This is covered in Meeting Analysis on page 112.

Just Say No

We covered learning to say no in chapter six. It is your right and prerogative to say no. If there is no value to you in attending a meeting, then don't attend it. If they need some information from you ask them what it is they need and send it to them. Or if all else fails ask them to deal with your input first and once you have delivered it leave the meeting.

Seven Deadly Sins

Eric Matson in his "Seven Sins of Deadly Meetings" cites some very senior people in large organizations admitting that their meetings were ineffective. The seven sins he identified were:

1. People not taking meetings seriously: arriving late, leaving early and spending most of their time doodling

2. Meetings lasting too long: they could accomplish twice as much in half the time

3. People drift off the topic: spending more time digressing than discussing

4. Nothing happens after the meeting: decisions don't get converted into actions

5. People don't tell the truth: there's plenty of conversation, but not much candor

6. Meetings always seem to be missing some important information, so they postpone decisions

7. Meetings never get better: people keep on making the same old mistakes

Hot tip

We will be looking at the antidotes to these problems in the next topic.

Good Meetings

We took a look at some of the reasons for bad meetings in the previous topic, so now let's look at what makes for a good, effective meeting.

Start on Time

Good meetings start on time, even if several people are not there. Even if the chairperson is not there, take the chair yourself and start the meeting. Then when the chairperson does arrive explain that you started the meeting on time so as not to waste other people's time and you will bring him or her up to speed on the items they missed after the meeting.

Short Meetings

I always schedule general meetings for a maximum duration of one hour and keep to it. Meetings are held to communicate, identify issues and make decisions, not to do detailed work. The chairperson should ensure the meeting sticks to the agenda and stop any discussion on how to do things. That should take place outside the meeting.

Occasionally meetings to develop or evolve a new product or process may require longer. They should be restricted to the required specialists and are often called workshops.

Finish on Time

In addition to starting on time, the chairperson should also ensure the meeting finishes on time, with any remaining issues noted for action (see action items below).

Stick to the Subject

At the start of the meeting the chairperson should outline the purpose of the meeting clearly together with any constraints. Then they should introduce each item for discussion and ensure that it is discussed effectively. If anyone drifts off the subject they should be brought back.

Action Items

Once a topic has been discussed, the chairperson should summarize any points of agreement and disagreement. Then establish the conclusions (final or intermediate) reached. They should then check the understanding and acceptance of the attendees and add any actions to the action items list, with the person responsible and a date for completion.

Open Culture

The chairperson should spot if anyone is not contributing to the meeting and attempt to draw out their opinions, viewpoints and experiences. If they really have nothing to contribute, why do they need to be there?

A good organization has an open culture that encourages people to speak up truthfully and admit any failures or issues. One of the best organizations I worked for had a great saying "It is better to ask for forgiveness than permission". That is the way to encourage an open culture and creativity.

Information Required

Along with (or as part of) the agenda for the meeting there should have been a note of any information that will be required at the meeting. That way the attendees will come prepared and decisions can be made, effectively.

Review Meetings

From time to time, and particularly when a meeting is going to finish early, the chairperson should review the meeting process with the attendees. Open discussion should ensue on the things that are effective and the things that might waste time. This is not 'navel gazing', it is process improvement. The chairperson should then feed the conclusions of this review back into the planning process for future meetings.

The Chairperson

It should come as no surprise that most of the things that make for a good meeting stem from the meeting chairperson. John Adair identified the following three steps to assess yourself:

1 List what you believe to be your strengths in chairing meetings (but only those corroborated by feedback from other people)

2 Then list five areas in which you would like to improve to overcome any present weaknesses

3 List the five lessons that you would like to bring out if you were planning to run an effective meetings training session for your group

Meeting Analysis

Most of the research published to date suggests that far too many people end up going to far too many meetings. This is not an effective use of your time so you need to establish which meetings matter and which do not. Which ones make an effective use of your time and which do not. Then you can make the basic decision about whether to attend a meeting or not.

Case Study

Many years ago I was working as a software manager for a large computer manufacturer. A new district manager was appointed, who held regular weekly meetings with their immediate reports. We would all gather in their office while they listed the items they wished to discuss. This would include stuff that was being passed on down the line from their manager together with their own needs and issues. No agenda was issued so we rarely had any idea of what we were going to be talking about in advance.

They would start out by telling us what they had been told to tell us and ask for any feedback to be passed back up the line. But any suggestions they disagreed with were quickly squashed. Then they would tell us their needs and issues and our role was to agree with their assessment and decisions. No tasks were ever allocated to individuals but we were supposed to use our initiative and do want they wanted. Within six months of their appointment every single one of us had moved on.

Information Gathering

What information do you need to gather in order to assess the effectiveness of a meeting and when should you do it?

To answer the second part of the question: the best time to do it is right after a meeting, while everything is still fresh in people's minds. Then to move on to the first part: meeting evaluations should meet several simple criteria:

- They should be short, say four to six questions

- Questions should be open-ended to invite honest opinions

- Provide feedback on the meeting's content and process

- Gather feedback about the effectiveness of the group

- Provide feedback about the leader's behavior in meetings

Hot tip

If you can't change your boss, change your job.

Information Analysis

For each meeting you analyze decide whether you should attend all meetings, some meetings (perhaps when specific topics are discussed) or none at all.

If you are going to reduce your attendance or stop altogether, provide feedback to the meeting owner so that they understand why you are dropping out. If phrased tactfully it may even help them to make their meetings more effective in future.

Meeting Analysis Sheet

The following is an example of a meeting analysis sheet:

Meeting:

Purpose:

Attended By:

Frequency:

Average duration:

What was good (content and process)?

What was bad (content and process)?

Meeting Effectiveness:

Leader's Behavior:

Return on Time Invested (ROTI):

Scale:
0 = No benefit received for the time invested
1 = Slight benefit but not equal to the time invested
2 = Benefits received equal to the time invested
3 = Benefits received greater than time invested
4 = Benefit received much greater than the time invested

Decision:

Other Comments:

Preparation

Effective meetings start with some preparation. Like any other form of communication the first thing is to establish what the meeting is for and what you want to get out of it. Use the following steps for preparing for a meeting:

1. Make sure you are clear about the purpose and objectives of the meeting, what you want to achieve and where you would like to be by the end of the meeting

2. Establish what type of meeting it needs to be: team briefing (to give instructions), information gathering, negotiation, decision making or possibly a combination of two or more types

3. Consider who you need to invite to the meeting in order to achieve its objectives and issue the invites in plenty of time to allow attendees to schedule it

4. Prepare the agenda, which should explain what each item is about, and issue it about a week ahead of the meeting with any supporting documents or information so the people attending can prepare in advance

5. Try to use diagrams or other forms of visual aid (one picture being worth a thousand words) and prepare them in advance of the meeting

6. Consider the use of any other props or equipment such as a projector, flip charts or documents

7. Select a suitable location for the meeting and think about the best layout for the room, lecture theatre, board-room, round table, etc.

8. If any attendees will need to make travel arrangements prepare directions and accommodation details

All of this will save time in the meeting and any time spent on preparation is seldom wasted.

Hot tip

Book the room for 30 minutes before the start time and 30 minutes after the planned end time to allow for issues and delays.

Agenda !

The Agenda

The agenda is the key item. It should list all of the topics for discussion and/or decision (indicating which is which). It should describe the subject so that people know what it is about rather than having vague headings that could mean anything. This allows them to prepare effectively for the meeting.

Meeting Preparation Checklist

The following checklist has been found useful in planning and preparing for a meeting:

Meeting purpose

Objectives (final or intermediate)

Identify who needs to participate

Prepare the agenda

Describe each topic for discussion or decision

Assign a time limit to each item

Check the agenda is realistic

Select the time and day for the meeting

Book a suitable meeting room and specify layout

Issue meeting invites

Confirm list of attendees

Issue agenda and supporting papers

Provide directions and local hotels for visitors

Prepare timetable for the meeting

Prepare attendance list if people are from different organizations

Organize any required catering

Prepare an introduction to welcome attendees and remind them of the objectives

Prepare any necessary materials and aids

Decide who will take minutes

Running the Meeting

Good chairmanship can save significant time during meetings and ensure they achieve their objectives. Your responsibility is to see that procedures are adhered to, the meeting is run effectively and that everyone has their chance to contribute. Be careful not to allow discussion to expand to fill all the available time!

Get There Early
This is a key bit of advice. Over the years I have arrived at a meeting room only to find: another meeting in progress, the room not arranged as requested, tables covered in dirty plates and cups, missing equipment and all manner of minor irritations.

Aim to arrive 30 minutes before the meeting is due to start and you will have enough time to sort out any issues. If nothing is wrong you will have a quiet half hour to prepare for the meeting or work on one of your other priority tasks.

Starting the Meeting
Start the meeting on time even if one or more attendees has not yet arrived. Delaying the start is discourteous to those who took the trouble to get there on time. Begin by welcoming the attendees and particularly any visitors. Consider asking people to introduce themselves if it the first time they have met, but not if it's a large meeting as it would take too long. Make sure everyone present knows the purpose and objectives of the meeting and what time it is scheduled to end at.

Controlling the Meeting
Once the meeting starts you will need to control it by introducing each topic in turn:

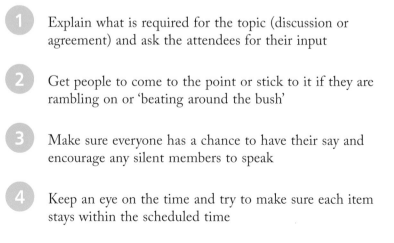

1. Explain what is required for the topic (discussion or agreement) and ask the attendees for their input

2. Get people to come to the point or stick to it if they are rambling on or 'beating around the bush'

3. Make sure everyone has a chance to have their say and encourage any silent members to speak

4. Keep an eye on the time and try to make sure each item stays within the scheduled time

5 After each agenda item summarize what has been decided and agreed and get the meeting's confirmation of it

6 If someone has been tasked with an action make sure they have understood and agreed what they will do and when they will need to do it by

7 Make a note of these last two steps to ensure they are recorded in the minutes

8 Later in the meeting remind people of the scheduled end time of the meeting and ask that they speed up their input if necessary

Hot tip

It's always better if you can get someone else to take the minutes so you can concentrate on chairing the meeting.

Closing the Meeting

Begin to draw the meeting to a close in sufficient time to allow you to make some closing remarks.

1 If necessary defer discussion or decision on the final one or two items on the agenda (these should have been non-critical topics)

2 Briefly summarize the results of each topic on the agenda that was discussed

3 Remind those tasked with actions when they are due for completion

4 Propose a date, time and location for any follow up meeting and check that the required attendees are available, but have alternative dates available

5 Thank the attendees and close the meeting

Failure to bring a meeting to a close on time risks people with other appointments leaving before the end. If they miss these last few steps there is a risk they will miss something critical and may not be available for the next meeting.

Follow Up

There are a number of follow on and follow up activities after the meeting is over.

Minutes of the Meeting

Minutes of meetings do not necessarily have to be formal. If it was an informal meeting they can just be issued as notes by email. If it was a formal meeting then the minutes should also be formal and produced as a document (which can still be issued as an attachment by email).

You should aim to issue minutes as soon after the meeting as possible. If someone other than you was tasked with taking notes and producing the minutes then let them know when you need the draft minutes.

In a business environment, minutes should be as brief as possible and not cover general discussion. They should only include salient points such as decisions made and actions agreed. They should include:

1. The title, date, time and place of the meeting

2. Names of those who attended the meeting and any apologies for absence (people who should have attended)

3. A heading for each topic on the agenda

4. Under the topic heading any conclusions reached, decisions made and actions agreed for the item

5. For any actions agreed: the name (or initials) of the person responsible for the action, with the date it is to be completed by

6. The time the meeting ended

7. The time, date and venue of the next meeting

The minutes should initially be issued as draft minutes to allow the attendees to raise any errors, omissions or queries. They can then be finalized and issued before the next meeting if they are to be formally accepted or approved at that meeting.

Minutes of a previous meeting should not be read out at the start of the next meeting. They have been circulated and any corrections made. So the chair should merely ask for confirmation of them.

Follow Up

Just distributing meeting minutes with assigned action items and due dates will not make things happen. Many meeting participants fail to even look at the minutes until the day of the next meeting. To make meeting follow-up work, you need to foster a culture of accountability so that people don't turn up at the following meeting without having completed their action items.

Action Items

In addition to entering the date of the next meeting in your diary, it is also a good idea to note the dates actions are due to be completed by. Then a follow up 'reminder' to the person responsible a few days before the due date can be invaluable in terms of the effectiveness of the group. Not to mention saving someone the embarrassment of having to admit they forgot something at the next meeting.

Tracking Database

If there are a lot of action items it might be worthwhile creating an action item database. It doesn't have to be a real database as a spreadsheet usually suffices. Add new action items following each meeting, update the status as things are worked on and mark them as closed once they have been completed. It can even be attached as an appendix to the minutes.

Thank You

When someone does complete their action it is worth sending them a quick thank you email (even if you had to chase them to do it). It reinforces positive behavior. It is also well worth sending a thank you email to anyone who contributed well to a meeting. Again this reinforces positive behavior.

Next Meeting

Finally start building up the topics for the next meeting right away as it will save time when you start preparing for it.

Hot tip

Review the list of action items regularly and make the whole team effective.

Summary

- Meetings can be one of the most effective means of communications but poorly-run meetings can be one of the biggest time wasters

- If your meetings don't start on time ask yourself why and what you can do about it

- Before scheduling a meeting ask yourself if you really need it or if there is a more effective way of achieving the same thing

- You probably don't need to attend all the meetings you go to so, when you receive an invitation, just ask yourself if you really need to go and, if not, say no

- Meetings can be ineffective if people don't take them seriously, they last too long, people digress, nothing happens after the meeting, people aren't honest in them, key information isn't available and people keep on making the same mistakes

- Good meetings start on time, they are short, they finish on time, points for action are agreed, there is an open culture, required information is provided, they review their own effectiveness and they have a good chairperson

- Analyze all the meetings you go to a couple of times a year and decide if the benefits you receive from attending justify the return on your time invested

- Good meetings start with sound preparation

- Get there early, control the meeting and finish it on time

- Keep the minutes of meetings as brief as possible and aim to issue them as soon after the meeting as possible

- Once you have issued the minutes of a meeting don't assume that everyone will read them and take the necessary actions

- Keep track of action items and give the people they are allocated to a little nudge before they are due; then thank them when they are done

- Remember to thank people who make positive contributions to a meeting to reinforce this behavior

9 Effective Delegation

Delegation can free up a lot of your time but it needs to be effective. In this chapter we explore delegation, the barriers to it and how to delegate effectively.

Delegation

In our quest for effective time management we have looked at using our time as effectively as possible and concentrating on the important tasks. But that means that some things won't get done unless we get someone else to do them. The process of doing that is called delegation.

Delegation becomes increasingly important the higher up the organization someone is, yet delegation is one of the key skills often missing in senior managers. Surveys have indicated that fewer than 15% of top managers are able to delegate effectively!

What Delegation Means

Delegation does not mean abdication or giving up responsibility for something; it simply means entrusting someone else to do something on your behalf.

You transfer some of your authority to them to enable them to carry out the necessary task and in return they accept some of the responsibility for carrying it out.

However, you still have the overall responsibility for the task being completed properly and therefore you still have to retain some control over it.

The concept seems to be fairly simple but in practice it seems to run into difficulties. Either people don't delegate at all or, when they do, they don't do it well enough.

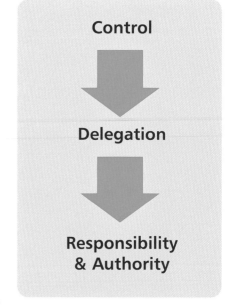

Control

Delegation

Responsibility & Authority

Why You Should Delegate

The primary reason for delegation is to free up some of your time. This will typically be by delegating routine or repetitive tasks to subordinates. The time that you gain from this will then allow you to concentrate on the important things that can add more value to the business.

Hot tip

Delegation is good for you and good for the business.

The secondary reason for delegation is that it helps to develop your subordinates by giving them a greater variety of work and entrusting them with more authority and responsibility.

Levels of Delegation

The level of delegation relates to the amount of authority you are delegating and the amount of freedom of action you are giving the delegate. Asking someone to do something and telling them exactly how to do it is not really delegation at all as you are not giving them any authority or freedom of action. Most experts on delegation identify four levels of delegation:

1 The lowest level of real delegation is asking someone to carry out a task for you but having a discussion with them on what they are proposing to do before making any final decisions. This might be suitable for delegating to an inexperienced person or one whose skills or ability to perform the task you are not yet fully sure of

2 The second level would be to delegate more authority to them and leave them to get on with the task but to keep you informed of their progress. This is showing more trust and confidence in their ability

3 The third level would be leaving them to get on with the task but with the option of referring back to you if they need any help or advice. This is showing even more trust and confidence in their ability

4 The fourth level is to leave them to get on with the task and just let you know how it worked out afterwards. This is showing total trust and confidence in their ability

What You Can't Delegate

There are two things you can't delegate:

- Accountability: as you will still retain the ultimate responsibility for the success or failure of the tasks you are delegating.

- Leadership: as you still need to develop your team and the individuals within it.

Why We Don't Delegate

Delegation does not necessarily come naturally to people. It is all too easy to find excuses not to delegate: It's quicker to do it myself, I don't have time to show them how to do it, I can do it better and so on. The fact is that delegation is a business decision.

When asked, people give many reasons for not delegating. The seven top reasons why senior managers don't delegate (with the possible real reasons added) are:

- It's too risky (I don't trust my staff)

- I enjoy doing things myself (I'm not prepared to share the fun things I do)

- I don't want time to sit and think (I like to feel very busy)

- It's a slow process (I'm not prepared to put in the effort)

- I like to be on top of everything (I'm a control freak)

- I fear my subordinates will outstrip me (I'm not confident)

- Nobody else can do it as well as I can (I'm over confident)

One unstated reason that applies in some organizations is the principle that knowledge is power. By keeping everything to themselves, people like to feel they will become indispensable to the organization.

The biggest barrier to effective delegation is often you. And these are the things that you might find yourself putting up as reasons for not delegating:

It Will Take Too Long

It will take longer to explain to someone how to do it than to do it yourself. That may be true for a one-off task but most things need doing more than once. Paradoxically, one of the main benefits of delegation is saving time but only in the long run.

Loss of Control

People who haven't learnt to delegate feel that they will be giving up control. They are frightened by the prospect of allowing someone else to complete a task for which they are responsible. Communicating with the delegate to check on their progress can help decrease this fear and keep you in control.

They'll Take the Credit

Some people are afraid that the delegate carrying out the task will then take the credit for it, when it was their idea in the first place. But part of the process of delegation is learning to let go and being prepared to share the credit with others. The better your team looks, the better you look.

I Enjoy Doing It

Sometimes you need to delegate tasks that you actually enjoy doing. But if the task is a low level, recurring task you shouldn't be wasting your time on it, even if you enjoy doing it. Teaching someone else how to do it and seeing them succeed should give you far greater enjoyment.

I'll Do it Better

You may think that you're the only person who can complete the task successfully. But how do you know, if you don't give others the chance to prove themselves? You may find out that you have a highly capable team if you can only learn to trust them.

I Won't Have a Job Left

Some people resist delegation because they think they will risk delegating themselves right out of their jobs. But in a good organization, people who effectively delegate and free up their time for business-critical tasks are seen as being ready to take on more responsibility and promotion. By delegating you will improve your effectiveness and your team's productivity and this should be obvious to everyone.

I Don't Trust Them

If you feel that you don't have faith in people to do the task correctly, ask yourself why. Is it because you've never tried it or that they don't have the necessary skills? If they don't have the skills then teach them. If you've never tried it, start by taking a small risk. Successes will then encourage you to delegate more.

They Don't Want to Do It

If your team members resist having tasks delegated to them, you may need to help them see the benefits in delegation for them as well as for you. It will help them to grow in their job as well and, once they start to succeed, they will be more willing to take on additional responsibilities. If they feel that they don't have enough experience, then give them the necessary training.

Hot tip

Delegation carried out effectively is good for everyone: the delegate, the delegator and the business.

What We Can Delegate

We saw in the topic on delegation that there are two things you can't delegate: ultimate accountability for the success or failure of the task you are delegating and leadership and development of the team. What you can delegate is almost anything else.

What to Delegate

It is best to start by delegating tasks that are not too important or time consuming to delegate. Routine or repetitive tasks are ideal candidates as they won't take too long to delegate and will start to free up your time right away.

If you haven't already done it, start a time log (as explained on page 28) and record how you spend your time for a couple of weeks. Then analyze the log and look for the lowest level task on the log. This is the one where you are just doing something out of routine. This will be the first task you are going to delegate.

Who to Assign

Next you will need to find someone suitable who you can delegate or assign the task to:

1   Start by looking at the existing skills and workloads of your team and see if there is someone who is relatively under-occupied, if so that is a good place to start

2   If not, look to see if there is somebody who has a skill or ability that could easily be transferred or developed into carrying out the delegated task

3   The third option is to identify the most talented member of the team and see if they ready to take on a new challenge. The chances are that if they are talented and you don't stretch them they are likely to leave anyhow

Having identified the task to delegate and the most appropriate person to delegate it to, you can now begin the process of delegation.

How Much to Delegate

The key decision is how much of the task you are going to delegate. Or to put it another way, how much control you want to exercise over the delegation.

We looked at four levels of delegation back on page 123 and these are sometimes referred to as the delegation continuum. But in reality there are many more than four levels and some pundits have even extended it to ten levels:

1. Follow these instructions precisely: this is a straight-forward instruction and there is no delegated freedom

2. Look into this and tell me the situation, then I'll decide: asking for investigation and analysis but no recommendation

3. Look into this and tell me the situation, then we'll decide together: enables the analysis and decision to be a shared process, which is helpful in coaching and development

4. Tell me the situation and what help you need from me in assessing and handling it, then we'll decide: gives them greater freedom for analysis and decision-making

5. Give me your analysis and recommendation and I'll let you know if you can go ahead: good delegation

6. Decide and let me know your decision but wait for my go-ahead: this level of delegation can be frustrating

7. Decide and let me know your decision, then go ahead unless I say not to: similar to the previous one

8. Decide and take action then let me know what you did and how it turned out: you trust them

9. Decide and take action, you don't need to check back with me: you would normally assess the outcome later

10. Decide where action needs to be taken and manage the situation accordingly, it's your area of responsibility now: this adds the responsibility to their job description

Authority

We looked at the relationship between authority, responsibility and control at the start of this chapter. In this topic we will expand on the process of delegating authority. Responsibility and control will be covered in the next two topics.

Delegation isn't just a question of allocating a task to someone, you also have to give them some of your authority so that they can carry out the task. As you will have seen in earlier topics, there is a wide range of varying authority that you can confer on the other person. The more experienced and reliable the other person is, the more authority you can delegate to them.

On the other hand, the more critical the task then the more cautious you need to be about extending a lot of authority and freedom. You will still be held accountable for the result.

Discussion

It is a good idea to ask the person you are delegating to what level of authority they feel comfortable being given. That way you can check that you are both happy with it. Some people can be very confident and others less so. You need to agree with them what level is most appropriate for them to get the job done effectively and with a minimum of unnecessary involvement from you. Involving the other person in agreeing the level of delegated authority for the task is part of the contract that you are making with them.

Delegating Authority

These nine guidelines can assist the process of effective delegation of authority:

1. Try to delegate tasks to people closest to the relevant work area as they are likely to be the ones who know the most about it

2. Make sure the delegate understands the desired outcome by describing what you want them to achieve

3. Explain why you have chosen to delegate this particular task and why you have chosen to delegate it to them. If it is also a part of their development process let them know that as well

4. Make sure they know exactly what responsibilities they are taking (covered in the next topic) and the level of authority you are delegating with any constraints and boundaries (such as your approval of proposed plans prior to their taking any action)

5. Don't forget that even though you are delegating a task to them the overall responsibility for it remains with you (this is covered in the topic on control)

6. Make sure you provide the right level of support to the delegate and communicate with them regularly

7. Focus on the results of the delegation and not on the way they are carrying out the task. They won't do it the same way that you might have done and letting them control their own process and methods will help to build their trust and confidence

8. If they hit problems, don't let them delegate the task back upward to you. Help them to identify possible solutions and choose the most appropriate. This will assist their development; taking the task back will do the opposite

9. Take time to review any of their work that is submitted to you as this is another opportunity for you to focus on their development

These nine guidelines for effective delegation of authority will result in a win-win situation for the delegate and the delegator. It will also bring benefit to the business.

Delegation Takes Time

Effective delegation does require an investment in time and commitment up front. But once you develop the necessary skills you will start to benefit from the time that you free up. Your team will develop their ability and commitment to the business. Your quality of life will improve as you can concentrate on the things that are most important to you and the business.

Responsibility

In the process of delegation you are delegating some of your authority to the delegate to enable them to complete the task. In return they have to accept a corresponding level of responsibility for completing it. Effectively the two have to balance one another.

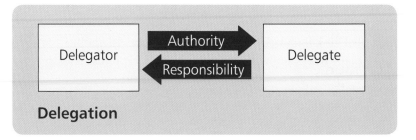

Level of Authority

As we saw in some previous topics, there can be a wide variance in the amount of authority you are delegating depending on the task and the person you are delegating it to. These levels of delegation are not an exhaustive list. So it makes sense to take some time to discuss and adapt the amount of responsibility you are expecting the delegate to take for completing the task.

Level of Responsibility

Try to be creative in agreeing the most appropriate level of responsibility with the person you are delegating to and ensure that they are comfortable with this. You will often find that people are capable of taking much more responsibility than you might think. The rate and extent of the responsibility they accept and the freedom to make decisions will help to determine their own development and advancement as well as your own.

Plan for Delegation

Plan ahead and don't wait for some crisis to unfold before you delegate. Identify what you can delegate and then decide what you will delegate. But before you decide to delegate something consider if it needs to be done at all or whether you can just eliminate it.

Try to delegate some good tasks as well as bad tasks and don't be tempted to keep all the interesting tasks to yourself. Also delegate complete tasks if at all possible, rather than just a small section of the task.

Hot tip

Don't wait for things to go wrong, if they do you won't have time to delegate effectively.

130

Who to Assign

Select the person who is most suitable for the task and not just someone who happens to be conveniently located. If they are not a direct report of yours discuss it with their line manager first.

Do respect their other work commitments and try to resolve any conflicts with them. Use the delegation as a way of developing the delegate. In general people will rise to meet your expectations.

Communication

Discuss the delegation with the person you wish to delegate to and get their input on the task. Give them enough information to enable them to carry out the assignment and clarify the outcome or results your are expecting them to achieve.

If the task is complex then document it as a back up to your description. Hearing it and reading it will increase their retention of the details. Confirm that they have received the details and that they understand what is being asked of them.

Set and agree the completion date with them and any interim checkpoint or review dates that you wish them to follow.

Carry out the hand-over in person so that you can resolve any further questions that they might have.

Finally, explain that you are delegating the necessary authority (covered in the previous topic) to them to allow them to accept the responsibility for carrying out the task.

Follow Up

Establish clear feedback criteria and diary note when things are due from them. Follow up things as they become due and give them any necessary advice or guidance if the task is starting to slip. If they hit problems, resist any attempts at upward delegation and provide help and advice instead.

Recognition

When they successfully complete the task give them the public recognition for it. Thank them and praise their work in front of the team and back it up in writing. The saying is "Praise in public and correct in private".

And remember that results that get recognized get repeated.

Control

As we saw in the previous two topics, the amount of authority that you delegate needs to be balanced by the amount of responsibility the delegate accepts and vice versa. But the process of delegation does not mean that you have no responsibility for the task any more. Quite the opposite, you are now responsible for the task itself and the delegate's completion of it. So the final piece of the equation is control.

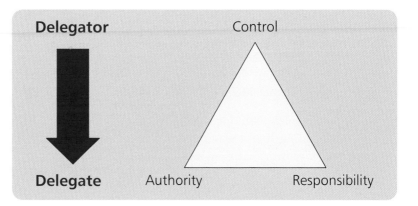

Delegator Control

Delegate Authority Responsibility

Control

Although you have delegated the task you still retain overall accountability for its successful completion. So you need to maintain a degree of control over the delegated task. The degree of control you need to maintain will be dependent on the ability of the delegate and your experience of delegating to them previously.

This was the basis of the examples of four and ten levels of delegation earlier in the chapter. But when you first delegate a task to someone you will not have anything other than gut reaction to base your judgement on so you will probably err on the side of caution.

Example

It might be useful if we look at an example of how this process could work out in practice:

1. You have reviewed your time log and identified that one recurring task that you could delegate is the weekly project progress report. You have identified one of the team and agreed the delegation with them

2. You have showed them some previous reports, explained the content and style you have used and asked them to use the same format to begin with

3. You ask them to bring you their first draft report so you can take a look at it before they issue it. When you see it you suggest that they should re-word a couple of sections, which might otherwise be confusing

4. They make the suggested amendments to the report and email it to you for a final check. You review it and spot a couple of typos so you email it back with these marked and ask them to make the corrections before they issue it

5. The following week they again send you their draft report and you are pleased to see they have taken on the points you raised the previous week

6. You feel that adding a diagram might improve the report and send it back suggesting they make the changes if they are happy to do so and issue the report

7. They make the change and issue the report

8. The following week they send you their draft report and you call them up to thank them and say it is fine to issue and not to bother sending you drafts in future unless they specifically want you to check or approve any content

9. The task is now fully delegated to them and you schedule a meeting with them in three months to review the on-going task performance

Stay in Control

By going through this process rather than just dropping the task on them and leaving them to sink or swim you have delegated the task in a controlled manner. You have encouraged them but shown them that you are still responsible for the end product.

Effective Delegation

Through this chapter we have explored the process of delegation, the obstacles to delegation, why we should delegate and the interrelationship between authority, responsibility and control. In this topic we will summarize all of these into a process for effective delegation.

The Act of Delegation

If it is a straightforward task or someone you have delegated to before, it could be a simple case of explaining what you want them to do. In which case explain it to them in a clear and concise way. Offer them any advice or guidance on to how to do it effectively. Finally get them to explain their understanding of the task to confirm that they have understood.

If on the other hand it is a more complex task or someone you have not delegated to before, you may need to arrange some training or coaching for them. The critical thing here is to remember that although you may be very familiar with the task, they are not. If necessary, break the task down into its component sub-tasks and take them through each of them, rather than trying to explain it all at once. Be patient with them, don't try to rush them and if necessary be prepared to repeat anything.

10 Steps to Success

Follow these 10 steps to effective delegation to ensure a successful outcome for you and the delegate:

1. Start by defining the task and confirming that it is suitable for delegation

2. Select the most suitable candidate for the delegate and ensure that you have selected them for the right reasons. Ask yourself what benefits they will get from taking on the task and make sure you know what you want to get out of it

3. Assess the delegate's ability by confirming that they are capable of carrying out the task, that they have a clear understanding of what has to be done and decide if they will need any training, coaching or mentoring to help them complete it

4   Explain the reasons why the task is being delegated and why you are delegating it to them. Explain how important or urgent it is and where it fits in regard to priorities with their other work

5   Tell them the required results, what you need them to achieve and how this will be measured. Question them to make sure that they have understood this

6   Discuss with them the resources they will require to complete the task in terms of their time, access to and time from other people and any budget requirements

7   Agree the deadlines for when the task is to be completed with any interim or review dates and confirm their agreement to accepting the responsibility for getting the task completed

8   Explain how you plan to exercise your control over the task and why you need to do so. Get their agreement to this and make sure they do not see it as a lack of trust in them or interference

9   In consultation with the delegate, communicate news of the delegation to all interested parties within your own area (and the wider organization if relevant)

10   On an on-going basis, communicate regularly with the delegate to provide feedback on their work and results (so they know how they are doing) and to check whether they require any support or advice

Review

Once the task is completed, review it with the delegate and discuss what went well and what did not go to plan. Thank them for their good work and work with them to resolve any problems for the future. Finally give them public credit for the success of the task if it went well but keep any problems or issues internal.

Hot tip

Share the credit for things that go well, you'll both gain.

Summary

- If we prioritize the things we do and only concentrate on the important tasks, some things won't get done unless we can delegate them to someone else

- Delegation does not mean abdication of responsibility, we still need to retain some degree of control over the task

- Delegation has two benefits: it frees up your time for priority work and helps to develop your subordinates

- The two things you can't delegate are accountability (you are still responsible for the task) and leadership

- People come up with many reasons for not delegating, often through fear or mistrust, but effective delegation is good for the delegator, the delegate and the business

- The easiest and best tasks to delegate are non-critical, routine or repetitive tasks

- Keep a time log for a couple of weeks and analyze it to identify the lower priority tasks you could delegate

- Find the most suitable person to delegate the task to and, based on their and your experience, identify how much authority you are going to give them to complete the task

- When delegating authority do it in a clear and controlled way and take enough time to do it right

- In return for the authority you are delegating the delegate must accept an equivalent level of responsibility for completing the task

- To stay in control of the task you need to set up regular progress review meetings with the delegate

- To begin with you will probably need to keep a close eye on what they are doing but as the task develops and you and they gain more confidence you can back off

- To delegate effectively: define the task, select the best delegate, provide any required training, explain the task and the results required, agree the deadlines and controls, communicate the delegation and let them get on with it

10 Home Working

More and more of us are now working from home. This chapter covers how to do it in an effective way.

The Home Office

Whether you call it home working, teleworking or telecommuting, more and more people are choosing, or being asked, to work from home either full time or for part of the time.

According to a recent Ipsos/Reuters poll about 20% of workers around the globe telecommute frequently; and around half of these work from home every day. Where I live in the South West of England over 15% of workers are now working from home, including me.

It sounds like a great lifestyle choice to start with. No more daily commute to work, dress how you like and have more time to spend with your family and so on. Most of these benefits are real but there are also some potential problems. We will be looking at these through the rest of this chapter.

Home Workers

So, what sort of people end up working from home? There are four main classes of people we can identify:

- People who are starting up or running their own business in a self-employed capacity

- Craft workers (people who make things) either in a self-employed capacity or working for an employer and are usually paid a piece-rate (that is they are paid a set price for each piece they make)

- Home-based traveling sales or technical people who spend most of their time with customers or clients either in a self-employed or employed capacity

- Full or part-time teleworkers, who have an office-type job but work from home, usually in an employed capacity

Whether you are employed or self-employed there are potential advantages and disadvantages to working from home. There can be cost benefits and cost implications. There can also be tax and insurance implications as well as benefits.

Scams

If you are working for yourself you need to be aware that there are a lot of sharks out there. Anything that asks you to pay money or provide your bank details up front is probably a scam.

Employment Rights

If you are a home-based employee your employment rights should be exactly the same as those of an office-based colleague. This includes your right to be paid at least any national minimum wage that applies to your country. Your employer also has a responsibility for your health and safety while you are working for them at home.

However you are also responsible for taking reasonable precautions while handling heavy goods, using electrical or mechanical equipment and using any hazardous substances or materials. And all home workers, whether employed or self-employed, should take care when working on their own for long periods of time.

Tax Status

Your tax status is not necessarily the same as your employment status. You could be self-employed for tax purposes but still be an employee for employment rights purposes. Your contract of employment should clearly set this out with your rights and responsibilities. If you are in any doubt get in touch with your local tax authority to clarify the position.

Working from Home

These are the four top tips for effective home working:

1. Create a dedicated office space with a clear separation between your work area and your home living area otherwise it is all too easy to get distracted

2. Set your working hours and keep to them but make sure you take adequate breaks

3. Limit your distractions by making sure your partner, family and friends understand that you are working from home, what this entails and that they are not to disturb you when you are working

4. Keep in touch with colleagues, co-workers or others working in a similar environment to keep up a professional circle of contacts

Hot tip

If there are other people in the house while you are working, a separate room for an office is not a luxury, it's a necessity.

Working Hours

If you are an employee your working hours will have been agreed in your contract of employment. This may be a fixed time such as 9 am to 5 pm or may be a more flexible 35 or 40 hour week. If you are self-employed you will need to decide this for yourself.

Hours of Work

Having decided or agreed the number of hours you are going to work per week, you then need to define what your working hours are going to be. This could be nine to five or an earlier or later start, to suit your lifestyle and other non-work commitments. But by defining what your hours of work are, you can then let everyone involved know when you will be working. This should cover friends, family and partner as well as your employer, clients and colleagues.

Breaks

Set fixed break times, particularly mid-morning, lunch time and mid-afternoon. It is all too easy to get stuck to your desk and get totally immersed in your work.

At least once an hour get up and stretch, walk about or make a cup of coffee. Go for a jog at lunch time or right after work, it will all help to keep you effective.

Separation

Make sure you have a clear separation between your working hours and your non-working hours. Treat home working the same as office working: don't take work into the home and don't take home into the office.

Starting Work

Aim to start work at the same time every day. Treat the days when you are working from home just like any other regular workdays. Get up, get dressed, have breakfast, go into your office and close the door. Sit down at your desk and start working at the usual time.

Structure the Day

Having a routine really pays off. It will help you to maintain a focus on your work. Your colleagues, clients and employer will also appreciate knowing where you will be at any particular time. It will also mean you can plan your day around any non-work activities such as taking the kids to school.

Other People

It is a really good idea to let your neighbors know what you are doing. Explain what it will mean to you and how it hopefully won't inconvenience them. Let them know about your working hours and if you do need quiet times, when these are.

Likewise you should notify your landlord, insurance company and mortgage lender so they are aware of what you are doing.

Effective Working

There are two main dangers to effective home working: working too many hours and not working enough hours. By defining your working hours and breaks and sticking to them, you should be able to stop yourself from working too many hours. By keeping a firm separation between work and home you should be able to stop yourself getting distracted and not doing enough work.

To be effective you need to strike the right balance between working and not working. Set your own deadlines and keep to them. It can be all too easy to switch off when you don't have the boss watching you any more.

If you've got important phone calls to take, make sure you have some peace and quiet, when you will not be interrupted by noisy family members or neighbors cutting the grass.

Let Them Know

Don't be afraid to put up a do not disturb sign:

I am Working

Please do not disturb except in an emergency

(I will be free at 12 noon)

Interruptions

The good news about working from home is that you won't now get the drop-in interruptions from your boss or colleagues. The bad news is that you might now get them from your partner, family, friends and neighbors.

Preventing Interruptions

After yourself, your friends and family are your greatest threat. So in order to limit interruptions and distractions, make sure they understand what your working hours are and what it means.

Use the following steps to minimize interruptions:

1. Differentiate between when you are working and when you are not by closing your office door and putting a 'do not disturb' sign on it

2. Explain to your partner and family that they are to take this 'do not disturb' sign seriously and not interrupt you

3. Make sure you have a different phone for work and home and don't answer your home phone while you are working, put it onto voicemail and pick up your messages when you stop working

4. Don't give your work phone number to friends or family and explain why if they ask you

5. If other members of the family or your partner are in the house and answer the phone, get them to say you are working and take a message

6. When you do stop for a break go and see them, thank them for respecting your work time and check for any messages

7. Deal with anything that needs to be dealt with while you are having your break and then go back to work

These steps enforced politely but firmly will greatly reduce the number of interruptions you get.

Dealing with Interruptions

While the steps listed opposite will greatly reduce the number of interruptions you get, they won't prevent them all together. Obviously if a family member has an accident or injures themselves and you are the only adult in the house you will need to deal with the situation but other non-critical issues can be handled differently.

Chapter seven covered interruptions in the office and the same points apply to dealing with interruptions in your home office:

1. Decide who and what you are prepared to interrupt your work for and make sure they know and understand why

2. When you do get interrupted stand up and ask them why they have interrupted you and how long it will take

3. Remind them that you are busy working and check if anyone else can deal with the problem

4. Ask them if they need an answer right away or if you can get back to them when you have your next break

5. Make a note of where you were when you got interrupted so that you can get back there once you have dealt with the interruption

6. If you are going to get back to them make a note of this too, so that you don't let them down

7. Listen to them politely but avoid small talk and ask them to come to the point if they are dithering

8. Be kind but firm with them and try to give them a few words of encouragement

Be considerate but be assertive about your working time. It is after all helping to pay for the roof over their heads, the food on the table and their vacations.

Staying in Touch

This topic is really the other side to the previous topic. While you need to get on with your work you also need to stay in touch with colleagues, your boss, customers and suppliers.

Don't Become a Hermit

Shutting yourself away in your office may be necessary to work effectively from home but not if taken to extremes. You are now more remote from the people you need to keep in touch with so you need to take steps to stay in touch.

Visit the Office

If you are employed, look for opportunities to visit your company head office. You need to stay in touch and have face-to-face meetings with your manager from time to time. Try and arrange meetings with other people for the same visit. Suggest having lunch with colleagues and co-workers. It's a great chance to bring them up to date on what you're doing and for them to do the same with you.

Visit Your Customers

Take opportunities to visit your customers' or suppliers' offices for the same reasons as above. Try to arrange face-to-face meetings from time to time. It does take longer but there are compensating benefits. Again consider having lunch with them and build your interpersonal relationships.

Conference Calls

Rather than doing everything by email, call people up on the telephone from time to time. But do agree the time and date with them in advance so you are not interrupting them. If you need to involve more than one person set up a conference call, these are easy to do using smart phones or conference facilities.

Use New Technology

Conference calls are even more effective if you set up a video link as well. Skype or one of the many 'free to use' video conferencing sites can provide excellent facilities. Encourage your organization to provide this type of facility.

If there's a company meeting and you can't be there ask if they can set up a video link for you and any other home-based workers. Again it all helps to keep you in touch with the wider world and your colleagues.

Self-Employed

If you are self-employed try to find some new colleagues, people who are doing similar things to you. You will be able to give each other ideas, feedback and support. When I first started my own business working from home a friend was doing the same thing. We provided each other with a lot of ideas, support and feedback. We even started to meet up for a drink after work on a Friday. I have also stayed in touch with two former colleagues and we meet up once a month on the last Thursday in the month so we can always schedule it in our calendars.

Other People

If you are working for yourself you will probably also have an accountant or bookkeeper. You will probably also have a solicitor and some form of IT support. Depending on the type of business you are in you may well have others. They can all be part of your people network and help you stay in touch.

Networking Groups

Depending on your line of business there will almost certainly be some sort of society or club you can join. With an ever increasing number of people working from home there are a growing number of self-help network groups springing up. If there isn't a suitable 'widget manufacturers' networking group, then start one up for yourself, you'll soon find other like-minded people.

Connect Online

You don't have to meet face-to-face if you don't want to as once again new technology comes to your aid. LinkedIn, Facebook, Yahoo and many more exist. Check out what's available and join in or start up a new topic or discussion group if there isn't a suitable one already.

Internet Cafes

WiFi hotspots are becoming much more widespread along with Internet cafes, hotels and pubs. Take the opportunity from time to time to get out and meet other people.

Get Out of Doors

When you do take a break get out in the fresh air. Go for a walk, jog or bike ride. Go to your local store to pick up a newspaper, a sandwich or some groceries.

Equipment

One of the most critical keys to working effectively from home is to make sure you have the right tools for the job. You've got a room sorted out for your office, now what are you going to put into it?

If you are employed, your employer may well provide you with much of the equipment you will need. If on the other hand you're starting your own business you may not be able to go out and buy everything right away, but do have a plan in place to get what you need as soon as you are able to afford it.

Chapter five listed the things you need to have in your office to be effective and guess what? They all apply to your home office. So let's start at the beginning:

Desk
First and foremost you will need a desk or table to work at. It doesn't need to be anything grand but it does need to be large enough to hold everything you need to work on at any one time.

Chair
No matter how tatty your desk, do invest in a good chair. You will be spending a lot of time sitting in it so it should be comfortable and provide good support for your back and position your body correctly for working at your desk. As well as comfortable to sit on it should be fully adjustable so that you can sit comfortably for some time. Ideally it should swivel and have castors so you can move about easily.

Visitor's Chair
Unless you have customers visit you at your home office it is not a good idea to provide a visitor's chair. See chapter seven on handling interruptions.

Storage
Work out what type of storage you will need: one or more filing cabinets, bookshelves and cupboards. When you finish work for the day or leave your office you should be able to clear everything away and leave a clean uncluttered desk.

Telephone
When working from home it is vital that the office, customers and suppliers can communicate with you at all times. You will need a

separate telephone line, with voicemail, for business use. You will be able to claim it as a business expense and you don't want your kids picking up a business call. When you finish work don't forget to divert calls to voicemail and don't be tempted to answer the phone if you hear it ringing, better still turn the ringer off.

Most people also have a mobile phone but again it's worth having a separate business mobile, which you can also turn off when you finish work.

Computer

Most home workers need a computer and again it should be a business computer. So treat it that way, password protect it and don't let the kids use it to surf the Internet! It could be a desktop or laptop or you might need both. If you just have a laptop, consider getting a decent-sized screen, keyboard and mouse. These can be connected through a docking station or just USB cables.

Internet

You will need an internet connection for email, video conferencing and general internet access. Get the fastest broadband connectivity you can as there is nothing worse than waiting ages for a large document or piece of graphic artwork to download.

Printer

The type of printer you need will be dependent on the volume of printing you do, your requirement for color and the print quality you require. Laser or Ink Jet printer will be determined by these factors but you should also consider the cost of supplies. While printers with a tricolor cartridge are cheaper to buy they are more expensive to run as you have to replace the cartridge when any one of the three colors runs out. Separate color cartridges are more economical in the long run.

Back Up

There is a wide range of back up material available from USB pens to high-capacity external drives and tapes. If you need to keep multiple copies of things then CD or DVD can be useful.

If you are employed, your employer may want you to synchronize your business files on their data store. This is also a good back up medium. Otherwise facilities like DropBox, Microsoft Hotmail and Windows Live can provide similar services.

147

Hot tip

Online storage is also great if you need to access files from different locations.

Summary

- More and more of us are working from home, either on a part time or full time basis and while this can bring some significant lifestyle benefits it can bring problems as well

- There are many different types of people working from home either on an employed or self-employed basis

- Employed home workers have the same rights as their office-based colleagues but also have a responsibility to take reasonable care

- Your tax and insurance status may be impacted by working from home and, if in any doubt, you should consult your local tax office and insurance company

- The top four tips for effective home working are: have a dedicated office, have clear working hours, limit distractions and keep in touch with fellow workers

- Decide on the number of hours you will work each week and then determine your daily working times but schedule in breaks so you don't get trapped at your desk

- Have a clear separation between your working hours and non-working hours, don't take work home and don't take home into your office

- You won't get so many interruptions from colleagues but your family and friends are now the threat so take steps to minimize this by laying down a clear set of guidelines for how you want them to behave

- You will still get interrupted by family so plan how you will deal with non-critical issues and be firm but fair, after all your work may be helping to pay for everything they enjoy

- You won't have so much contact with colleagues so plan how you will keep in touch with them and build up network and support groups

- Your office is just the start; to be effective you need to arrange a desk, office chair, storage, a business phone, computer, broadband internet access, a suitable printer and back up data storage (either on back up media or on line)

11 Stress

Stress is a major health hazard today, but by taking steps to reduce it, you can be happier and more effective.

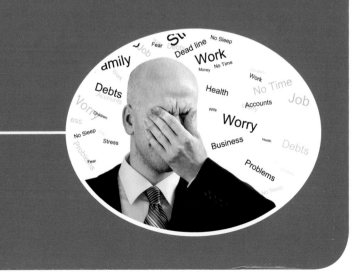

What is Stress?

Stress is a term in common use today but it is difficult to define exactly. The word originally derived from the Latin word 'stringere', meaning to draw tight. In simple terms, stress is the feeling of being under too much mental or emotional pressure.

Major Health Hazard

Stress is without a doubt one of the major health hazards in the workplace. Having too much work to do or not feeling in control of it can cause stress. Too much or even too little responsibility can cause stress. Feeling unable to discuss problems or issues with your manager can cause stress. Working in a bad environment (too hot, too cold or too noisy) is another recognized cause of stress. Work-related stress can lead to sickness and absenteeism and this can have a detrimental effect on work colleagues.

Pressure

We are all under a certain amount of pressure in our work and some people actually enjoy the sensation. But pressure can turn into stress if we feel unable to cope with it. People have different ways of reacting to stress, so a situation that feels stressful to one person may in fact be motivating to another.

Besides work, many of life's other demands such as relationship and money problems can also cause stress. I once read somewhere that the three most stressful things in life are changing your job, moving home and getting married. I managed to go out and do all three at the same time and, despite some consequent stress, managed to survive!

Results of Stress

When you feel stressed, no matter what the cause, it can begin to affect everything that you do. It not only impacts on how you feel, but also how you think, how you behave and even how your body functions. It can result in sleeping problems, sweating, loss of appetite and difficulty in concentrating.

Stress-related Illness

While stress itself is not an illness, it can cause serious illness if it is not tackled. It can result in a wide range of conditions from rashes and skin disorders, circulatory disorders, digestive problems, through to anxiety or panic attacks, insomnia or difficulty in sleeping, depression, nervous breakdowns, heart attacks, strokes and even suicide.

Recognizing Stress

It is important to recognize the symptoms of stress in yourself as early as possible. This should help you to figure out ways of coping with it rather than turning to unhealthy coping methods, such as drinking or smoking.

Spotting the early signs of stress may also help prevent it getting any worse and resulting in serious complications, such as high blood pressure, anxiety and depression.

Symptoms of Stress

Stress can give rise to a wide variety of mental or emotional symptoms that can affect:

- How we feel - Typically people who suffer from stress can feel moody, bad-tempered and easily irritated. They may be agitated, anxious, worried, uptight, overwhelmed or lonely. They may even lose their self-esteem and confidence.

- How we think - When we are suffering from stress, our minds can start to race from one subject to another and we may have difficulty concentrating. We can become forgetful, have poor judgment and feel more negative or pessimistic than usual.

- How we behave - Drinking or smoking more and taking drugs to help us relax can be symptoms of stress. We might have difficulty sleeping, start biting our nails or begin eating more or less.

Stress often comes about gradually and the mental and emotional stress symptoms described above are usually the first signs that someone is not coping. It is important that these stress symptoms are recognized early and dealt with.

Advice

The British National Health Service web site (along with many others) has some excellent advice on managing stress. They say that while there is little you can do to prevent stress, there are many things you can do to manage stress more effectively. They list learning to relax, taking regular exercise and adopting good time management techniques.

Don't forget

Adopting effective time management will help you reduce stress and lead a happier life.

Signs of Stress

The danger with stress is that we only recognize the signs of it when it has become acute and the person is going through some sort of crisis. Alcohol dependency, chronic absenteeism or some form of nervous breakdown usually indicates this.

So make sure that you look out for the early signs of stress and deal with it before it becomes a crisis. Ask yourself if you ever get stressed at work and if so what sort of things cause it. Look out for the symptoms not just in yourself but in your team and colleagues.

Warning Signs

Some of the main physical symptoms of stress include:

- Heart pounding faster, blood pressure rising, breathing quicker, senses becoming sharper

- Feelings of giddiness or fainting

- Constant tiredness, disturbed sleep, insomnia or reliance on sleeping pills

- Recurrent colds or other infections

- Increased smoking, use of alcohol or other drugs

- Muscles tightening and feeling tense

- Needing to go to the toilet more often

- Frequent crying or desire to cry

- Indigestion, headaches, nausea

- Impotence or frigidity

- Incessant worry

- Irritability

- Loss of appetite or over-eating

- Nervous tics or nail biting

- Tendency to sweat for no obvious reason

Any one or more of these symptoms can be a warning sign of stress in yourself or other people.

Hot tip

Watch out for these signs of stress in yourself and your team.

Reaction to Stress

These symptoms of stress are completely natural. In fact they are our body preparing to flee from or fight the perceived danger that prompted the stress symptoms.

These physical changes help your body to protect itself from danger by increasing your strength, stamina, speed of reactions and helping your mind to focus on the situation. It is not unusual to experience some of these symptoms after a sudden shock like being involved in or narrowly avoiding an accident.

Stress Triggers

The pressure that leads to stress can come from work and our private lives and a certain amount is quite normal. Unfortunately it can build up. There are a number of factors which can cause a significant level of stress, particularly if the person concerned is already under a lot of pressure at work. These are some of the more obvious stress triggers:

- The death of a spouse or partner

- The death of a parent, child or close friend

- The break up of a marriage or close relationship

- Serious illness or injury

- Any major changes at work

- Loss of your job

- Moving home

- Getting married

Positive Stress

In addition to the negative triggers above, physical symptoms of stress can also be experienced with positive stress. This could be making a major sales presentation, standing up to give a talk to a group of strangers, taking part in a major sporting event or even having to go up onto a stage to receive an award.

Stress that gives us problems is, however, negative and it can affect our bodies over a longer period of time giving rise to other physical complications such as the warning signs opposite.

Causes of Stress

We looked at some of the triggers that can cause stress in the pervious topic. Many of these were not work related but it is interesting to consider the 12 most common known causes of stress:

1   Time pressure and deadlines: we have seen earlier in the book how trying to do too much just makes things worse, when what you really need to do is to use your time more effectively, prioritize your work and learn how to say no

2   Work overload: is again the result of taking on too much work and this again can be dealt with by prioritization, delegation and learning to say no. We looked at how to reduce a work overload and how to prevent it happening again in chapter six

3   Inadequately-trained subordinates: if your people are not sufficiently trained, then you won't be able to delegate work to them. We looked at the whole process of effective delegation, including the need to provide support and training for your team in chapter nine

4   Long working hours: this is the main effect of ineffective use and management of your time, which we looked at together with what you can do about it in chapter two

5   Attending meetings: this will be a problem if you attend all the meetings you get invited to rather than selecting the ones that are important and declining the others. We dealt with this in chapter eight

6   Demands of work on private and social life: this is usually the result of having a work overload and consequently working excessive hours, rather than prioritizing what really matters, including your private and social life

7   Keeping up with new technology: while we have not specifically covered this as a problem so far, it is increasingly something we all have to do. If it's a problem

then you need to schedule in some training or learning time into your schedule

8 Holding beliefs that are in conflict with those of the organization: this one is tricky as it has nothing to do with the effective use of your time. If it is actually causing you stress then you are probably working for the wrong organization and chapter thirteen may be of some help

9 Taking work home: again this is a symptom of poor time management, lack of prioritization, lack of delegation and the inability to say no, all of which have been covered earlier in the book

10 Lack of power and influence: this is the feeling that people either won't listen to you or they ignore what you have to say. If someone is in this situation they may well be in the wrong job or are seen as being ineffective

11 The amount of travel required by work: effective time management may help with this but at the end of the day if you are not happy with the amount of traveling you have to do in your job, then the answer is simple: find another job

12 Doing a job below your level of competence: you feel you are capable of doing something more challenging but your employers either don't or there isn't a more challenging job available. The answer is to talk to your boss and find out which it is and whether there is anything in the interim they can do to give you more responsibility. If not start looking for a more challenging job within or outside of the organization

The majority of these most common causes of stress can be addressed through more effective time management, which is what this book is all about. The remainder come down to the fact that you seem to be working for the wrong organization or boss, in which case you should plan to change your job.

Hot tip

Plan to keep abreast of new technology, it's important to your job.

Don't forget

If you can't change your boss, change your job!

Stress Reduction

In the previous topic we looked at twelve common causes of stress in the workplace and suggested that more effective time management would help with most of them. In more extreme cases the people concerned were probably in the wrong job. But in addition to effective time management, there are a lot of other things you can do to help with stress.

Understanding Stress

Stress is what happens to people as a reaction to pressure. The pressure can be from an external source or it can be internal (such as wanting to be seen to perform well in your job). People experience stress when there is an imbalance between the demands placed upon them and their ability to cope with these demands. Symptoms include anxiety, irritability, tearfulness, headaches, stomach problems, sleep difficulties and general ill health. But most of these symptoms are transient and will disappear when the cause of the stress is removed.

However, as we have seen, longer term exposure to stress can lead to serious problems such as high blood pressure, heart disease, depression, substance abuse and even suicide.

Support Network

Having a good support network can help you deal with stress at work, but taking measures to reduce the source of the stress will be better for your long-term health.

Seek Medical Advice

Seeking medical help is always good advice if you have a problem and stress is a problem. If you are suffering from any of the more acute signs of stress, anxiety and depression the first step should always be to consult your doctor. You need to make sure there is nothing physically wrong with you. If there is, your doctor will prescribe the necessary treatment.

Take Steps

After that you can then embark on a stress-reduction program. These seven steps were recommended by John Adair:

1. Take action: the symptoms are an early warning sign, so identify the underlying stress factors and do something about them. Anything is better than brooding so take some exercise to get your mind onto happier things

2 Express your feelings: and don't bottle things up, find a way of talking to a friend, partner or even a doctor, priest or counsellor, they are, after all, trained to listen

3 Review your priorities: step back and take a good long look at your values and priorities, make sure you balance work with play and try and have some fun in life. Change the things that you can change

4 Accept what cannot be changed: there will always be some things that you can't change, so try to be wise and philosophical about it

5 Put your own experience to good use: by reflecting on your negative experience you should start to feel more sympathetic to other people and their difficulties. This will in turn make you feel better as well

6 Check your time management skills: and set some realistic and achievable targets for improving your time management. Identify the areas where you have the most to gain. Accept the areas where you are weak and try to use the techniques in this book to improve them. Make sure you allocate time to the important tasks rather than concentrating on the urgent ones and work methodically, doing one task at a time

7 Count your blessings not your afflictions: concentrate on the here and now, don't dwell on the past or worry about the future. Find five things you can be thankful about and think about them

The Results
When we are less stressed we are more productive, take less time off work, have fewer accidents and are generally happier. This results in better morale, which in turn makes the workplace a more pleasant environment. Working in a pleasant environment means we are happier with life overall and our private and social life will also improve as a result.

Don't forget

Objectives should be SMART (Strategic, Measurable, Agreed, Realistic and Timed).

157

Summary

- Stress is one of the major health hazards in the workplace today and stems from people being under too much pressure at work or outside work

- While stress itself is not an illness it can lead to serious conditions if it is not tackled: skin disorders, sickness, nervous breakdowns, heart attacks and even suicide

- Stress can not only affect how you feel, it can also affect how you think and behave

- While you cannot prevent stress altogether, you can help to manage it by learning to relax, taking regular exercise and practicing good time management techniques

- There are many signs of stress you can look for, such as: increased blood pressure, giddiness, tiredness, recurrent infections and increased use of alcohol, tobacco and drugs

- The symptoms of stress are often your body reacting to perceived danger by preparing for flight or fight

- There are some major stress triggers: the death of a partner or close relative, break up of a relationship, major changes at work, loss of a job, moving home or even getting married

- There can be positive causes of stress through having to do something in front of strangers or taking part in a major sporting event

- Most causes of stress reported by managers can be addressed by effective time management but some indicate they are in the wrong job

- You need to start out by understanding what stress is and how the symptoms can disappear if you remove the cause

- Having a good support network can be a real benefit and seeking medical advice is essential if your symptoms are acute

- Seven steps to stress reduction from John Adair are: take action, express your feelings, review your priorities, accept what can't be changed, put your experience to good use, check your time management skills and count your blessings

12 Life and Everything

In this chapter we look at health, wealth, happiness and all the other things outside of work that matter in life. By looking after yourself you will maximize your effectiveness and what you get out of life

Health

This chapter was originally going to be called Life, the Universe and Everything (in memory of the late Douglas Adams) but it wouldn't fit. I somehow think he would have liked that.

While not at first directly associated with time management, if we want to be effective, we need to live a balanced life and that is what this chapter is all about. The first three topics are health, wealth and happiness, so let's begin with health.

Health

The World Health Organization defines health as a state of complete physical, mental and social well-being (sometimes referred to as the health triangle) and not merely the absence of disease or infirmity. But a number of other factors also influence our health, including our background (genetic inheritance and family upbringing), lifestyle and the economic and social conditions in which we live. The choices we make about our lifestyle will have a significant impact on our health. The key to this is balancing work with play, sleep, eating and exercise.

A report from Canada identified three interdependent fields as the key determinants of an individual's health: lifestyle, environmental and biomedical. This is what they said:

Lifestyle

Studies suggest that we can improve our health through exercise, getting enough sleep, maintaining a healthy body weight, limiting alcohol use and avoiding smoking. Failure to make these lifestyle decisions can lead to poor health, illness and premature death. So the results are very much in our own hands.

Environmental

This covers all external matters related to our health over which we have little or no control. Factors such as clean water, unpolluted air, adequate housing, safe communities and roads have all been found to contribute to good health. By contrast a lack of recreational space and natural environment leads to lower levels of personal satisfaction and higher levels of obesity, linked to lower overall health and well being.

Biomedical

This covers all aspects of physical and mental health as influenced by our genetic make-up or the traits we have inherited from our parents. These too play a role in determining the state of our health through the predisposition to certain diseases and health conditions, as well as the habits and behaviors we develop through the lifestyle of our families.

So that's the background, now let's look at what you need to do about it.

Maintaining Health

Achieving and maintaining your health is an ongoing process for which you have to take responsibility. When you get ill, medical science is there to help you with all manner of trained specialists but as the old adage goes, prevention is better than cure.

As we saw in the previous chapter, prolonged stress may have a serious impact on your health and it has been cited as a factor in cognitive impairment, depressive illness and disease. Good health is not just about not being ill, it is about being happy and feeling whole from both a physical and mental point of view. Being healthy means taking care of yourself to prevent illnesses or to speed recovery following illness. Taking care of your health means doing things that make you feel good, eating the right way, enjoying exercising and having a job you enjoy doing.

Working Life

Balancing your work life with your social, personal and active life and making room for each will contribute towards an altogether more rounded and healthy existence. This means that spending time with friends and taking exercise will mean you are more likely to perform well at work.

It also means that the environment in which you work should be as pleasant as possible, given the nature of your work. It should be clean, tidy and safe to maximize professionalism and respect for colleagues. You should know exactly what your job role is and feel you are valued for the job you do. You should have the correct amount of responsibility to enable you to carry out your job

Investment

Any time that you spend sick is wasted time (or poor quality time at the very best) so you should invest in your health. When you feel good you will be more relaxed and confident and in turn that will make you more effective at whatever you do.

Hot tip

Take care of your health and it will repay you with a better life.

Wealth

Money may make the world go round but it (or the absence or even too much of it) can also produce a lot of problems. I once had a very profound thought, there are only two people in the world who cannot say "At least there are people who are richer and poorer than me" and I would not want to be either of them!

Charles Dickens probably produced the most succinct summary where Mr Micawber advised the young David Copperfield:

- Annual income 20 pounds, annual expenditure 19 pounds, 19 shillings and six pence, result happiness.

- Annual income 20 pounds, annual expenditure 20 pounds and six pence, result misery

In short young man, live within your means. But often, as Mr Micawber found, that is not so easy as it sounds.

Balancing the Books

In basic bookkeeping terms you have to do what Mr Micawber said and not what he did. You need to balance the books by money management. The very rich can afford to pay other people to manage their money for them and there is a lot of wealth hidden away from the tax authorities in various unsavory tax havens. The rest of us don't have that luxury or lack of scruples so you have to do it for yourself. What you need to do is simple: balance your expenditure with your income.

Income

Most families have one or two main sources of income with possibly some other investment or other more minor income. This bit is easy, we all know what our total annual income is, as we have to declare it to the tax authorities each year. Unfortunately expenditure is not so straightforward.

Expenditure

We all know that we spend the money, hopefully less, but often more than our annual income each year. But what do we actually spend it on? It's quite an emotive subject and one person's luxury is another person's necessity.

Warren Buffett challenged prospective investors to embrace his frugal ideology: make sure every single item of expense is worth making. In other words challenge what you spend money on.

Hot tip

In today's money that's: $80,000, $80,100 and $79,900 respectively.

We can't all be in Warren Buffett's league but we can use his frugal ideology: before spending money on anything carry out a cost benefit appraisal. Money management can mean gaining greater control over outgoings and incomings in a personal as well as business perspective. Greater money management can be achieved by establishing budgets and analyzing costs and income.

Establishing a Budget

A budget is a record of how much money you have coming in (your income) and how much money you have going out (your expenditure). By knowing this you can take control of your money and plan for the future.

Budgeting can help you see exactly where your money goes. By listing all your income and spending you can gain a clear picture of your finances. You can:

- Spot overspending and paying for things you no longer need

- Live within your means by adjusting your expenditure

- Work out what you can afford, as a quick look at your budget can tell you if you have enough money to pay for things

- Plan for big expenses by putting money aside each month

- Save for the future by using any spare money to invest

Working out your Expenditure

Make a list of everything you spend money on. It is likely to be a long list so group areas of spending together. For example, housing (rent, mortgage repayments, property tax), services (electricity, gas, water, sewage, broadband, phone), housekeeping (groceries, cleaning, window cleaner), motoring costs (car depreciation or repayments, road tax, fuel, servicing), entertainment (television, games, dining out) and luxuries (vacations, magazines, wine, beer, cigarettes, chocolates, treats for the kids). Add up how much you spend on these a year and then calculate how much you need to set aside for these in your monthly budget. If it's more than your income, work out what you can do without.

One final thought, with the exception of a mortgage, don't borrow money to finance things you can't afford now. You will end up in debt and your biggest item of expenditure could be debt servicing.

Hot tip

Borrowing money should be your very last resort, not your first.

Happiness

The smiley face is now probably the best known symbol of happiness. Wikipedia defines happiness as "a mental or emotional state of well-being characterized by positive or pleasant emotions ranging from contentment to intense joy".

Many people and groups have tried to define happiness and how we might attain it, but put simply, happiness is a state where we feel content with the quality of our life. It is not about money, as long as we have enough to live on, although a Harvard Business School study found that spending money on others actually makes us happier than spending it on ourselves.

Abraham Maslow

The psychologist Abraham Maslow, developed his Hierarchy of Needs theory and motivational model and published it in 1954 in his book "Motivation and Personality". It is still valid today and widely used for understanding human motivation, management training, and personal development. The following diagram is normally used to illustrate the model:

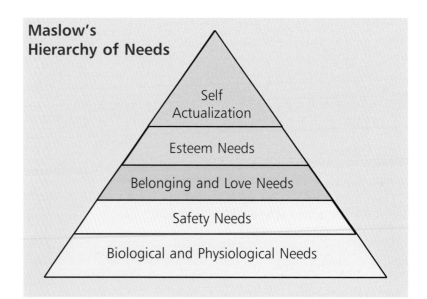

Maslow's
Hierarchy of Needs

Self
Actualization

Esteem Needs

Belonging and Love Needs

Safety Needs

Biological and Physiological Needs

Hierarchy of Needs

Maslow's ideas were formulated around the responsibility of employers to provide a workplace environment that would enable and encourage employees to fulfil their potential (self-actualization). We are all motivated by our needs. The most basic of which are inborn and hereditary. Maslow's Hierarchy of Needs helps to explain how these needs motivate us.

Maslow's Hierarchy of Needs states that we must satisfy each need in turn, starting with the first, which deals with the most basic needs for survival itself. Once the lower order needs of physical and emotional well-being are satisfied we can move on to the higher order needs of influence and personal development.

Conversely, if anything that satisfies a lower order needs, is taken away from us, we stop being concerned about the higher order needs and focus instead on the missing lower order need.

The five levels of need form five basic steps to self-fulfillment and happiness:

1. Biological and Physiological needs: first you must satisfy your basic needs for life: air to breathe, food to eat, drink, shelter, warmth and sleep

2. Safety needs: having satisfied these basic needs you then need to satisfy your need for safety and security: protection from the elements, law, order and stability

3. Belonging and Love needs: once you are secure you need to satisfy your need to belong and be loved through friends, family, relationships and your work group

4. Esteem needs: Once you feel you belong and are part of a group you can begin to develop your self-esteem, achievement, independence, status, prestige and managerial responsibilities

5. Self-Actualization: finally once you have developed your self-esteem, you can begin to realize your personal potential, self-fulfillment and personal growth

Hot tip

If you have any issues with a lower order need, getting it sorted out should be treated as your top priority.

Sleep

As we saw in the previous topic, sleep is one of the basic needs of life. Some people do seem able to get by on very little sleep, but most of us are more effective when we get enough sleep.

How Much Sleep

Studies have shown that the average adult needs between seven and a half and nine hours of sleep per night (children and teenagers need even more). But according to the National Institute of Health, the average adult sleeps less than seven hours per night. That means that the majority of us do not get nearly enough sleep, which means we will not be fully effective.

Sleep Deprivation

If you are getting less than eight hours of sleep each night, then you may well be sleep deprived. Some symptoms of this are:

- Needing an alarm clock to wake up on time in the morning

- Finding it difficult to get out of bed

- Feeling sluggish in the afternoon

- Getting sleepy in meetings or warm rooms

- Getting drowsy after big meals or when driving

- Falling asleep watching television in the evening

- Feeling the need to sleep in at the weekend

Sleep Debt

Sleep debt is the term used for the effect of sleep deprivation. A large sleep debt can cause mental, emotional and physical fatigue. It results in a diminished ability to perform high-level cognitive functions. Clearly you are not going to be fully effective if you are suffering from sleep deprivation and have a large sleep debt.

Some of the negative effects of sleep deprivation are:

- Fatigue, lethargy and a lack of motivation

- Moodiness and irritability

- Reduced creativity and problem-solving skills

- Inability to cope with stress

Beware

If you build up a sleep debt it will eventually catch up with you.

- Reduced immunity, frequent colds and infections

- Concentration and memory problems

- Putting on weight

- Impaired motor skills and increased risk of accidents

- Difficulty in making decisions

- Increased risk of hypertension, diabetes, heart disease and other health problems

Sleep Advice

If you suffer from insomnia see the section on Moonlighting on page 58. Otherwise the following suggestions are thought to help with making the most of your sleep:

1. Relax your mind: practice a simple breathing exercise for ten minutes: breathe in through your nose for three seconds, using your abdomen not your chest, breathe out for three seconds, pause for three seconds and repeat

2. Regular exercise: another good way to improve your sleep but don't do it close to bedtime as exercise produces stimulants that stop the brain from relaxing quickly

3. Create a calm bedroom environment: your bedroom should be for sleep, so no television or computer

4. While it's fine to have a nightcap, too much alcohol close to bedtime can make you restless

5. Avoid caffeine in the evening: caffeine is a stimulant that can stay in your system for many hours

6. Eating a heavy meal or spicy foods too close to bedtime will also interfere with your sleep

7. Get into the habit of going to bed and waking up at the same time each day, even at the weekend

Diet

The mere mention of the word 'diet' has the power to strike fear into grown men and women. It is probably fair to say that most of us will have gone on a diet at least once in our lifetime if not more often. Diet fads come and go and they all seem to work for the first week or two. But as soon as we go back to our usual habits, the weight just comes right back.

Most of us are aware that smoking causes cancer and heart disease but the advice is still ignored by a large percentage of the population. Other advice on what to eat and drink changes with the seasons but we all know that we should:

- Eat a balanced diet with lots of fresh fruit and vegetables

- Eat vegetable and fish protein in preference to red meat

- Reduce fat and dairy products

- Watch the alcohol and caffeine

Sensible Diet

The idea of a good, balanced diet is that it should give you sufficient calories to replace what you use through exercise. If you need to lose weight then you need to decrease the calories you consume, increase the calories you expend through exercise or a combination of both.

The US Department of Agriculture developed a pyramid model that outlines all the components necessary for a balanced diet based on strict scientific principles.

The pyramid consists of five food groups, which are grains, vegetables, fruit, dairy, meat and beans, plus a portion for essential oils. Starting at the base and working our way up the pyramid, the recommended daily amounts are:

- six portions of grains, which includes pasta, rice, bread and cereals; with a portion being defined as a slice of bread or half a cup of cereal

- five portions of fruit and vegetables; with a portion being an apple, banana or half a cup of cooked or raw vegetables

- three portions of milk and milk derivatives; with a portion being a cup of milk or two ounces of cheese

- two portions of protein: white meat, fish and in moderation, red meat and eggs with a portion being two to three ounces

- one portion (tablespoon) of oil, preferably Omega 3 or 6

To be effective, a sensible diet should involve lifestyle changes, if needed. There is an achievable balance between both taking care of the Earth and taking care of yourself, your body and your health. Once you have found this personal balance, your diet should be easy and sensible in fulfilling your needs.

Variety
A healthy diet should contain the right amount of calories and nutrients to prevent nutritional deficiencies and excesses. As different foods provide different nutrients, even within the same food group, variety in your diet is important. Eating several different foods from each food group will provide necessary nutrients, as well as keeping your diet interesting.

Environmental Considerations
Our diet depends on the environment functioning for the growth of crops and animals. By being conscious of the environmental impact of your diet you can help to avoid problems in the food system. Buying local food products, buying organic food and limiting meat consumption will all help the environment.

Organic Food
Buying locally-produced organic food does help the environment but is there any real difference between organic and conventionally produced food? While there is no clear scientific evidence of any significant difference, what does differentiate organic food is the way in which it is produced. The fewer artificial chemical fertilizers and pesticides, the more room for livestock to roam freely and higher welfare standards.

This suggests that purchasing organic food is more of a lifestyle choice than a necessity. It attracts devotees in the same ways that some people choose to become vegetarian. There will always be fears of long term health effects and environmental disasters, so we feel that by contributing in our small ways, we might make a difference towards the greater good. It seems that organic food, recycling, re-using your plastic bags and turning the lights off, are all symptoms of an ever changing modern mentality.

Hot tip

Become more aware of what you eat by keeping a record for one week.

169

Exercise

If you are too busy to take exercise, then you are too busy. Exercise generates energy and improves your health. It also balances out some of the pressures of work.

Why Exercise?

For many, the word exercise conjures up a ghastly image of a row of people sweating away on exercise machines in a gym. But in practice, while the gym suits some people, there are plenty of other options available to anyone that wants to keep fit and healthy, or lose a bit of weight. Not to mention the fact that gyms are big business and not cheap.

Physical exercise and aerobic exercise (such as running, cycling, swimming or brisk walking) in particular, is the best type of exercise. It will help you stay healthy, release tension, burn off a few calories and generally make you feel happier. There is no need for a full workout as, with a bit of ingenuity, 30 minutes' exercise every day will be enough to make you feel energized and content. The key is that whatever exercise you do, make sure it's fun or you won't keep it up!

Exercise Every Day

Build in some exercise every single day. It could be walking, running or cycling, but equally well gardening or cleaning the house. They are all exercise. Take the dog or the children for a walk in the park. Take a ball or a frisbee and have a bit of fun in the fresh air. It's all good exercise.

Some other ideas include:

- Don't take the elevator, walk up the stairs

- Get off the bus one or two stops early and enjoy a walk

- Don't slump at your desk at lunch time, take a walk before you eat your lunch

- When you go shopping, park further away from the entrance

Once you get started you will be able to find more and more opportunities for exercise and you will start to feel good about it.

The Benefits of Walking

Most of us spend far too much time sitting: at our desks, while driving, watching the television and so on. Get up and walk. You

Beware

Most gyms take money from your bank every month, whether you use the gym or not!

don't need any special clothes (although sensible shoes help) and it doesn't cost any money. It doesn't require any expensive gym membership and you don't have to be trained how to do it, you already know so get up and go.

Walking (like cycling and swimming) is a low impact form of aerobic exercise. It does not put so much stress on your joints as jogging or running. But it is a cardiovascular activity, so walking is good for your heart and lungs, as well as improving muscle tone and reducing body fat. Regular walking can reduce the risk of disease, relieve stress, help you sleep and improve your mood. Walking can easily be incorporated into your daily routine. It will make you fitter, could save you money in transport costs, is good for the environment and will make you feel happier.

Start in the Morning

Exercise first thing in the morning is a great way to wake yourself up and energize yourself for the day ahead. Walking, jogging, a bike ride or swimming, for 20 or 30 minutes, will leave you feeling great. Walk the kids to school. Or what about walking or cycling to work in the morning? It's much better than sitting in a traffic jam or being in a crowded bus or train with people coughing their germs all over you.

A Gentle Start

If you feel you need a slightly more gentle way of starting to take more exercise then things like yoga, pilates or stretching may be options to get you started. They are all beneficial in their own right and will help to get you back into a regular exercise routine. They should all raise your pulse rate and make you feel slightly out of breath.

Yoga is a discipline that aims to improve the health of your body and mind. A yoga teacher will direct you through a series of positions that will exercise your body and leave you feeling relaxed. Pilates is similar and will improve your muscle tone and your posture by a series of low impact repetitions. Again it will support your body and mind working together. Stretching is something that doesn't require a teacher as there are plenty of books on the subject and it can easily be done at home.

No matter what form of exercise you choose, make sure you do a little bit every day, enjoy it and keep it going for best results.

Hot tip

Start gently and build up the amount of exercise you do as your level of fitness grows.

Take a Break

"All work and no play makes Jack a dull boy" is a very old saying and one that is very true. In addition to sleep, diet and exercise, you also need to take breaks from work to refresh your body and mind and increase your effectiveness. You also need to have a bit of fun and enjoyment. So we all need to take a break from work every so often.

The Problem

It is all too easy to find yourself becoming a workaholic. The amount and pressures of work never seem to stop growing. Work hard by all means and work effectively but don't just work longer and longer hours. The next thing you know you will be working at weekends. Then you will be too busy to take a holiday and, if you were forced to take one by your nearest and dearest, you would probably be thinking about work the whole time. It doesn't sound much of a life and it is certainly not effective time management.

You probably spend about one third of your time sleeping and we covered the importance of that earlier in this chapter. You also spend around one third of your time (and hopefully no more) working. That leaves the other third of your time for leisure, relaxation, friends, family and hobbies. What you need to do is balance the work with leisure and recognize the need to take a number of breaks.

What Do You Enjoy?

Think about your life outside of work. What are your main hobbies and interests? What do you really enjoy doing? What gives you a real buzz and leaves you feeling happy? These are the things you should be finding time for to balance out the hard work. So now is the time to do something about it:

1. Make a list of the all things that bring you pleasure, that you would really like to do

2. Next prioritize them by how much enjoyment you would get from doing each

3. Now start at the top of the prioritized list and begin to schedule these activities into your plan for the next week, month or year depending on the activity

These things are just as important as work if you are going to manage your time effectively, so give them the same priority. So now let's take a look at when and how you take a break from the pressures of work:

Once an Hour

While you are working at a desk, get up and stretch or walk about once an hour. You only need to do it for a couple of minutes and it will stop you getting stiff from sitting in the same posture for too long. The same holds true if you are on a flight or a long train journey. It will also refresh your mind.

Lunch Break

Take a proper lunch break for half an hour at the very least and preferably an hour. Don't spend it sitting at your desk reading. Get out and take some exercise before eating. It will recharge your batteries and make you much more effective for the afternoon.

Leave Work

At the end of every working day you leave work and go home. Even if you are working from home you should go through this transition. So don't take work home with you, either mentally or physically, leave it all in the office, wherever that is.

Friends and Family

Get your priorities right and spend time enjoying yourself with your friends or family. Take up a new hobby, join a group, play ball in the park, play tennis, go bowling or just do something different. It will all help you to unwind and forget work so that you can return to it feeling good about it in the morning.

Take a Vacation

A vacation or holiday is a wonderful way to recharge the mental batteries. It doesn't matter if you go with friends, family, a partner or even on your own. And if you do go on your own, you might like to consider a group holiday like walking, sailing or skiing, you'll end up with like-minded people and probably make a whole bunch of new friends.

Get away for at least a week or two once or twice a year. Leave all your worries behind (needless to say do not take work with you) and have a great time. You will return to work feeling great and ready to take on whatever life has to throw at you.

Hot tip

Build some fun into your life, it will make you a better person.

173

Meditation

I can already hear some of you groaning at the thought of meditation. It's for mystics and weirdos, not me. But wait, because meditation is not as weird as it sounds and it can have some impressive results from a little practice. It is also growing in popularity. A recent US Government study found that nearly one in 10 adults had practiced meditation in the past year. And that was a significant increase on their previous study.

What Is It?

Meditation is a process where practitioners induce an inner form of deeper consciousness through controlled breathing and focusing the mind or attention on one specific point. Meditation has been practiced since antiquity, often as a component of a religious tradition or belief. But it doesn't have to be, it can be practiced on its own, without the incense or any other trappings.

The good thing about meditation is that any philosophical or religious beliefs are not important. It doesn't matter if you have them or not, as meditation is purely about consciousness. Meditation gets us into our inner reality and can be practiced by people of different religions or no religion with equal benefit.

Benefits of Meditation

Studies have found that people who meditate are happier and healthier than those who don't. People who meditate sleep better and may even need less time sleeping thanks to the recuperative results of meditation. Meditation is also credited with providing its practitioners with improved mental and emotional health. It can rid our minds of subconscious feelings of anxiety, anger, depression, fear and sadness. It is said to produce a perfect mental and physical balance. People who meditate are said to have more stable relationships and be satisfied and content with their lives.

Meditation has been used in clinical settings as a method of stress and pain reduction. There have been many cases where meditation has been seen to reduce and even reverses illness. There are even claims that meditation can extend the practitioner's life span.

I Don't Have Time

A lot of people quite like the idea of meditation, but feel they don't have enough time. What we have been saying throughout this book is that you can invest time as well as spend it. Meditation is something you should consider investing your time in as it will improve your effectiveness. If you feel you don't have enough time, try watching less television, try going to bed 30 minutes earlier and getting up 30 minutes earlier. Meditation clears the mind and makes the rest of the day more productive. Nothing can beat the feeling of inner peace it brings and meditation can give you inspiration. If you have peace of mind, your work will be more enjoyable and more productive.

Simple Meditation

Meditation is not only very good for the body and mind it is also very easy. Don't eat before meditating and don't meditate lying down as you are quite likely to fall asleep if you do. You don't need to sit in the lotus posture, a straight backed chair is fine. You can meditate at any time but it is probably best in the early morning as it sets you up for the rest of the day:

1. Sit quietly for 20 minutes, relaxed, breathing slowly, with your eyes closed and be still

2. Focus your mind on your center (solar plexus) and concentrate on one single thing, your breathing

3. Don't worry if you mind begins to wander, to begin with let it go where it wants

4. As you develop you can bring your mind back to your center or whatever other single thought you chose to meditate on

5. When you have finished, open your eyes slowly and bring your concentration back to your surroundings

6. Stand up slowly, stretch and feel at peace with the world and your surroundings

That's all there is to it. Afterwards you will feel more alert and less tense. It is particularly good if you are suffering from stress.

Learn to live your life one day at a time, you can't change the past so let it go and make tomorrow better by living well today.

Hot tip

Give meditation a try, you'll be amazed how good it can make you feel.

Summary

- You can improve or maintain your health through a combination of exercise, getting enough sleep, maintaining a healthy body weight, limiting alcohol use and avoiding smoking

- To be effective you need to balance your working life with your social, personal and active life

- Manage your money by establishing a budget of what your income is and what expenditure you can afford

- Happiness is a state where you feel content with the quality of your life and it results from satisfying a series of needs from basic survival to realizing your personal potential

- The average adult needs between seven and a half and nine hours of sleep each night but on average gets less than seven

- Make the most of your sleep by going to bed and getting up at the same time every day, having a calm bedroom and learning to relax before going to sleep

- To maintain your health and body weight, you need to eat a balanced diet including grain, fruit, vegetables, dairy products, protein and healthy oils

- To stay healthy you need to build in at least 30 minutes of exercise five times per week

- You don't have to go to the gym for exercise as running, cycling, swimming and walking briskly are all excellent forms of aerobic exercise you can do anywhere and at any time

- You can easily get more exercise by walking up stairs, getting off the bus a couple of stops before your destination and getting out in the fresh air at lunch time

- If you don't fancy running then walking, yoga, pilates and stretching are all gentler ways of starting

- Build breaks into your life to balance out the demands of work and don't take work home

- To really feel good try a spot of gentle meditation, it may turn out to change your life

13 Personal Action Plan

In this final chapter we look at putting it together in a personal action plan, plus 20 top time management tips.

My personal development

The Future

If you have worked your way through this book you should have a (possibly quite large) list of the things that you want to do or change in your life. Hopefully you have already started on some of them. But now it's time to put them all together into a personal action plan, starting with your long term plan. Where do you want to be in five years' time?

What Do You Want?

This is the big one, what do you really want out of life? If you haven't already done so it's time to sort out your personal objectives, where you want to go and what you want to do. This was covered back in chapter three, but at that stage we were focusing on work objectives. If you have already completed that exercise, go back and review it in light of the things we covered in chapter twelve. It's time to add in your personal objectives so they really do cover everything you want from life including health, wealth and happiness.

Remember that objectives need to be SMART so review them to make sure they are realistic. There is no point in setting an objective that is unrealistic or unachievable as you will only end up demotivated. Finally set the time target for when you want to achieve each one by. Again make sure it's a realistic and achievable time frame.

Don't forget

Objectives need to be SMART: Strategic, Measurable, Agreed, Realistic and Timed.

Money

To achieve your personal objectives you will need to have enough money coming in to meet or exceed what you will need to spend to meet them. Assuming that you don't already have that much coming in, then how are you going to increase your income by the required amount?

Changing Your Job

The first thing to consider is promotion: are there better-paid jobs within your current organization that you can aspire to? If so what do you need to do to get promoted? Consider your skills and abilities; do you need to develop any of these to make yourself more suitable for the desired position? If the answer is yes then these factors should go into your personal development plan.

Then consider your visibility: are you seen by the people who matter as someone who is suitable for promotion? You need to think about your behavior and the way others see you. Do you act in a mature way, are you seen as positive and willing to take on new challenges? Are you seen as an effective time manager? Do you deliver what you commit to on time and in a competent way? If you answered no to any of these questions then, again, you need to include any required behavioral changes in you plan.

If you currently have a good boss, these are all things that should feature in your annual performance review. Your boss should work with you to help you achieve your goals.

Changing Your Employer

If you do not believe there are opportunities for you to develop as you wish to within your current organization, then you need to change the organization that you work for. This means moving to a new employer or working for yourself. If you choose moving to another employer, then add this to your plan so that you can go about it in a controlled way. But be careful not to burn your bridges by telling your colleagues what you are planning to do. If you decide to start your own business then add this into your plan but don't rush it, these things take time.

Starting Point

Today is the first day of the rest of your life (usually attributed to Charles Dederich) so take it as your starting point. Where are you today in relation to where you're going? You need to be clear about this so you can track your progress towards your objectives. Describe how you spend your time now: how much time you spend working, sleeping and at leisure (relaxing, exercising, enjoying yourself and so on):

1. If you haven't already done so you need to keep a time log (as covered in chapter two) to record how you spend your time at work for a couple of weeks

2. You also need to do the same thing for how you spend your leisure time

3. Then summarize and analyze it adding the cost of all the work activities (as covered in chapter one)

Costing the things you spend your time on will help in the next stage, deciding if it is worth you continuing to do it.

Hot tip

Knowing the value of your time will help you to prioritize your work.

179

Personal Development

Wikipedia defines personal development as the activities that improve our awareness and identity; develop talents and potential; build human capital; facilitate employability; enhance quality of life and contribute to the realization of dreams and aspirations.

Put more simply, personal development covers the things that you do in order to achieve your long term goals. The types of benefit that personal development can bring to your working life are:

- Clearer understanding about the kind of life and work you want to pursue

- Greater self-confidence in the choices you make

- More confidence in the skills, qualities and attributes you bring to your career of choice

- Being in a better position to compete for jobs

- Being better able to discuss your skills, personal qualities and competencies with your employers

- Better problem-solving and planning skills

- Developing the positive attitudes and approaches associated with successful professional life

And the benefits it can bring to your personal life are:

- A better understanding of yourself and what makes you the way you are

- Being in a better position to make decisions about your personal aspirations

- Greater understanding of your needs and how to meet them

- Greater awareness of the unique contribution you can make

- Developing a positive, forward-looking approach to life

Many organizations now expect their employees to understand their own performance and development. Whilst some employers may offer training, it is increasingly common for employers to expect their employees to manage their own performance. Any time devoted to understanding what influences your own performance is time well spent.

Hot tip

Take responsibility for your own performance and development.

Continuous Professional Development

Employees are often expected to show a commitment to their own continuous professional development. This means seeking out information, training courses and events that will keep your skills and knowledge up to date. Knowing how to learn, and how you learn best, will be invaluable in the workplace.

Personal development is hard work. It takes time, consistency, and patience. But it will put you on a path of practical, positive growth towards achieving your long term goals. Personal development will help you to:

- Improve your ability to connect with others

- Build your motivation and discipline

- Take command of your life, and learn to make decisions

- Summon the inner strength to take action in spite of fear

- Create a daily routine that gives you a sense of flow

- Build a career you're truly passionate about

- Achieve financial adequacy

- Adopt health habits that empower your physical body

Personal Development Plan

Personal development planning means thinking through questions such as:

- What do I really want to achieve from life?

- What kind of person do I really want to be?

- Am I clear about my personal goals and ambitions?

- Am I making the right decisions to get me to where I really want to be or am I just hoping it all will work out?

Your personal development is not a quick fix, it is something that happens over a period time. It should be a key part of planning for your future. When you have identified where you want to be in five years' time; you can plan your personal development to take you there. Then each year review your progress against your plan to monitor your progress.

Developing Your Plan

Once you have identified your long term objectives (where you want to be in five years) and where you are today, you can develop a plan for how you are going to get from here to there.

Getting From A to B

Now it's time to get out the broad brush. You know where you are starting from today (A) and you know where you want to get to (B) so what will you need to do in order to get there? What will you need to change? Don't worry about how you are going to change things yet, just identify what you will need to change.

We looked at this in chapter two and it's probably a good idea to make two lists. One for the things you want to stop doing and one for the things you want to start doing.

Stop Doing

The type of things you might want to stop doing are:

- Trying to do too much
- Working late too often
- Taking work home
- Saying yes too readily
- Procrastination and other time wasting
- Spending time on things that aren't important
- Dealing with things in a haphazard way
- Going to too many meetings
- Being late for meetings
- Missing deadlines
- Being too flippant or non-serious at work
- Forgetting birthdays and anniversaries
- Being out of control
- Feeling stressed

Some of these might not apply to you and there may be many more that do but use this list as a starting point.

Start Doing

Having identified the things you want to stop doing you can now go positive and identify the things you want to start doing, things such as the following:

- Plan your working day and leave work on time

- Take breaks at least once an hour

- Prioritize important work over urgent work

- Learn how to say no and mean it

- Deal effectively with interruptions

- Check if you really need to go to meetings

- Make your meetings effective

- Review how you spend you time regularly

- Delegate more effectively

- Sort out your workspace and filing systems

- Communicate more effectively

- Be more effective on the telephone and email

- Develop any skills required for your personal development

- Be more positive at work

- Talk to your boss about your ambitions

- Start your own business

- Take up a new hobby

- Get 30 minutes of exercise every day

- Spend more time with your friends and family

Mid Term Plan

Again many of these might not apply to you and you may well have a number of others that are not listed, just use it as a starting point. Prioritize these and the things you are going to stop doing and feed them into your personal action plan for the coming year.

Don't forget

We looked at developing a mid term plan for the coming year back in chapter three.

Top 20 Tips

These are the top 20 tips for effective time management. Some are fairly easy to do, others are more difficult. If you are looking for inspiration for your mid term plan consider these:

1. Identify and document your goals for what you really want to achieve in life

2. Create a long term plan for what you want to achieve over the next five years

3. Make two lists of all the things you want to stop doing and all the things you want to start doing

4. Develop a mid term plan from your long term plan and change objectives to cover what you want to achieve over the next year

5. Keep an accurate time log for two weeks, then analyze it to find out what you are really spending your time on and check if it is in line with your plan

6. Keep an on-going prioritized action list for all the important tasks you want to complete

7. Create a day plan for what you are going to spend your time on each day, including prioritized tasks, breaks and some time for dealing with the unplanned

8. Review what actually happened compared to your plan at the end of each day, update your task list and prepare the next day plan

9. Once a month, review your progress against your mid term plan

10. Don't procrastinate, if you need to make a decision make it and move on, if it turns out to be wrong just learn from it and use that knowledge next time

11 If you've got too much work to do, then do something about it; learn how to delegate effectively, the more you do this the better you will get at it

12 Get your personal workspace and filing systems organized and tidy so that you work effectively in your office

13 Stop attending unnecessary meetings and make sure that any meeting you do go to is run effectively

14 Only check your email two or three times a day and sort it out into action, information, reading and junk

15 Don't allow the telephone to run your life, be prepared to divert it to voicemail when you are busy

16 Work smarter, not harder, by prioritizing, planning and breaking work down into manageable chunks and remember the Pareto Principle: concentrate on the most important 20% of anything

17 Deal with interruptions effectively and learn how to say no, politely but firmly, and mean what you say

18 Stay aware of how you are spending your time during the day as compared to how you planned to spend it

19 Identify any things that cause stress in your life, and work at trying to eliminate them

20 Take care of yourself in terms of your health, diet, exercise and leisure activities and start enjoying yourself by scheduling in things you like doing

So that's the top 20 tips for effective time management. When you are able to tick all those boxes you are making the most effective use of your time and enjoying life.

Don't forget

All work and no play makes Jack a dull boy.

Summary

- Work out your personal objectives, what you really want to achieve in life and where you want to be in five years' time, this is the start of your long term plan

- Remember that your objectives should be SMART: Strategic, Measurable, Agreed, Realistic and Timed

- If you want to get on and earn more money you will need to change your job through promotion, changing employer or starting your own business

- If you haven't already done so, keep an accurate time log for two weeks to establish exactly where you are today and how you spend your time

- Costing up your time is an excellent aid to helping you prioritize your work

- Personal development is the process of developing yourself in order to be able to meet your long term goals and should be a key part of planning for your future

- As well as developing any required skills, personal development can help you become more confident, put you in a better position to compete for jobs and develop a positive approach to life

- Identify all the things you want to stop doing in your work and personal life

- Then identify all the things you want to start doing or doing more of in your work and personal life

- Your long term plan, personal development needs and behavioral changes you want to make should all get fed into your mid term plan for the coming year

- Make sure you include your personal and non-work needs, as these are just as important

- Check the top 20 tips for effective time management and include any of these that are relevant in your plans

- Remember to take care of yourself and make sure you have some fun in life

J

K

I

L

U

V

W

Y